PRAISE FOR THE AUTHOR

"Cyndy Porter is a transformative force in the realm of personal style and image consulting. Her unique blend of artistic insight and scientific precision sets her apart, making her an invaluable guide for anyone seeking to redefine their personal and professional presence. Cyndy's ability to help individuals unlock their confidence and express their authentic selves is nothing short of inspiring. Her dedication and expertise shine through in every aspect of her work, making her a true beacon of empowerment and transformation."

—Danny Iny, CEO, Mirasee

"Cyndy is a personal branding consultant like no other. Cyndy's work comes from a deep place of purpose, intention, and with the aim to propel those she works with into their own greatness. Diving deep into the stories we tell ourselves, Cyndy helps guide a journey of learning who we are and how to forecast that to how others see and view us. Her work is marvelously evergreen, and my time spent with her still echoes in my confidence, how I show up, and in my business success."

—Naomi Hattaway, Founder and CEO, Leaving Well

"Cyndy Porter's impact on my life has been life-changing. With her specialized background in photography, style, design, and business, she has taught me how to show up personally and professionally in a way that authentically communicates my core values. While I have worked with several stylists over the years, no one comes even close to Cyndy—she is simply the best of the best!"

—Lorraine Hightower, Certified Dyslexia Advocate and Consultant

"Cyndy Porter has the vision for knowing how to make every individual feel and look their best!"

—Tina Johnson, CEO, CEO Consulting Group

"Cyndy has taught me to authentically align who I am with how I present myself to the world, translating to how I dress personally, professionally, online, and at speaking engagements. I now feel fabulous every time I get dressed, I get compliments everywhere I go, and people even stop me on the street. I owe it all to Cyndy; she truly lives her mission of helping people see their beauty inside and out!"

—Risa Ganel, Founder and CEO, Together Couples Counseling

"Cyndy made it easy to quickly find the right clothes and shoes without breaking the proverbial bank. It's great knowing I now have a wide selection of looks to choose from, all of which look great."

—Opher Ganel, PhD

"I am blind and was recently divorced. I was uncertain about how to update my wardrobe to be more social. I felt awkward not knowing what colors would work for me and what styles were appropriate. Cyndy worked very closely with me, and together we did a complete closet makeover. The improvement was immediate. With pictures of my new look, I saw a tenfold increase in interest on dating sites.

—John Bailey, Computer Programmer

"Cyndy has helped me completely revamp my image to reflect my own personal brand, and in the process improved my self-confidence."

—Ashley Loyd, CFO

"I highly recommend working with Cyndy to bring your professional brand and your personal style to a whole new level of awesomeness!"

—Jill Cruz, Founder and CEO, Wyn Weight Loss

"Amazing. I love how Cyndy embraces her clients' authentic selves. She cares about her clients and exceeds expectations over and over. She's made such a positive impact on my personal style, my business, and my life. The *best*, 100% worth the investment!"

—Hannah Serota, Principal, Creative College Connections

"I've always been clueless about fashion, but Cyndy has a remarkable talent for making style accessible and fun. Her guidance and practical tips have been a game changer for me. I'm so grateful for her incredible ability to help even the most fashion-challenged individuals like myself!"

—Tania Pilkinton, Marketing Executive, Marriott Vacation Club

"You will be so impressed with the quality, personal attention, and amazing results Cyndy gives."

—Beanie Silverstein, Retired

"Cyndy's guidance as a personal stylist has not only refined my style, but also empowered me to coach other women and men. Her passion and expertise have inspired me to help others to find their confidence and beauty. I am forever grateful for her mentorship and unwavering support. She embraces the individuality in each person and helps her clients to become who they truly want to be. Thank you, Cyndy, for making women feel beautiful and the world a better place."

—Kristin Alice Loé, Nurse and Image Consultant

YOUR ULTIMATE *Style* BLUEPRINT

Cyndy Porter

MIRASEE PRESS

5750 Avenue Notre Dame de Grace
Montreal, Quebec
H4A 1M4, Canada

www.mirasee.com

Copyright © 2025 by Cyndy Porter

All rights reserved.
This book, or parts thereof, may not be
reproduced in any form without permission.

Illustrations were created by Shayna Davis (shaynadavispro@gmail.com)
unless noted otherwise.

Photography was created by the author.

Hardback ISBN: 979-8-9916600-1-3
Paperback ISBN: 979-8-9916600-0-6
E-book ISBN: 979-8-9916600-2-0

LCCN: 2025900659

Printed in the United States of America
1 3 5 7 9 10 8 6 4 2

This book is dedicated to all the people who struggle to show up in the world with poise and confidence; my clients, who teach me how to help others and to be the best version of myself; my husband, Jack, and son, Steven, who believe in me and support my many endeavors; and Zoey, my beautiful husky/lab, who is always sitting at my feet, encouraging me to do my best work.

Contents

INTRODUCTION...I

Section I: Crafting Your Visual Identity: The Art of Personal Branding...................1

   1: The Power of Self-Confidence and Personal Image............3
   2: How Your Appearance Shapes Others' Opinions.................9
   3: The Essence of Personal Branding and Style....................15
   4: Defining Your Brand Identity..21
   5: Artfully Expressing Your Personality and Values................33

Section II: The Art of Dressing for Your Unique Features...........55

   6: Embracing Your Unique Shape and Form........................59
   7: Balancing Act: Styling Your Body's Unique Proportions....85
   8: Elevating Your Look with Color..119
   9: Artistry in Detail: Line, Scale, Texture, and Pattern..........137
   10: Enhancing Your Features: Face Shapes and Makeup....153
   11: Hair Harmony: Finding Your Ideal Style and Stylist.........173
   12: Complete Your Look: The Art of Accessorizing..............185
   13: Wardrobe Mastery: Building a Closet Full of Clothes That Inspire You to Be Your Best..209

CONCLUSION...223
EPIGRAPHS..227
ENDNOTES...231
ABOUT THE AUTHOR..237

INTRODUCTION

Why fit in when you were born to stand out?
—Dr. Seuss

Are you an entrepreneur, a job seeker, or a professional looking to move up the ladder? You may simply want to look better for yourself and others. If so, this book is for you. Setting yourself apart from the crowd, showcasing your strengths, and attracting attention to your unique point of view are critical for success. How you look can support you in these goals. It can also get in your way.

I struggled to feel comfortable in my skin for much of my life. It was like carrying a backpack full of bricks everywhere I went, weighing me down with self-doubt. When I learned how to dress to communicate my personality and showcase my best features, I became more confident, carried myself differently, spoke up more often, and took more risks. Success followed.

I became an image consultant and wrote this book because I am passionate about helping people look and feel radiant, confident, and even magnetic.

My approach is unique. Many stylists can help you look terrific. But you are 100% dependent on them for the looks they create. Instead, I

YOUR ULTIMATE STYLE BLUEPRINT

teach you to do it for yourself. You won't just learn what to buy and wear but why it's right for you. And you'll come to understand how art, brand marketing, science, and psychology can be combined to create an image and style that build confidence and attract success.

Whether you are heavyset or model-thin, straight or LGBTQIA+, this book will provide you with everything you need to have a closet full of clothes that you love, the confidence to show up for every occasion of your life feeling your most attractive, and the ability to grab the attention of others.

Let's get started on this journey together.

Section 1

CRAFTING YOUR VISUAL IDENTITY: THE ART OF PERSONAL BRANDING

There's power in allowing yourself to be known and heard, in owning your unique story, in using your authentic voice.
—Michelle Obama

Your personal brand is more than just a logo or a tagline. It encompasses every facet of your being, from your self-confidence to how you express yourself through your style and demeanor. It is like your unique signature—a combination of your personality, values, lifestyle, and preferences. It expresses who you are both online and offline, and it plays a crucial role in how others perceive and remember you.

Throughout this section, we'll explore the elements of personal branding, from the power of self-confidence and perception to the essence of defining and creating a cohesive and authentic personal brand that resonates with others. By infusing authenticity and intentionality into every aspect of your presentation, you forge a genuine connection with your audience and leave a lasting impression.

Whether you're a seasoned professional looking to refresh your brand or a newcomer seeking a memorable first impression, this section provides the insights and inspiration you need to craft a visual identity that truly reflects who you are and what you stand for.

Chapter 1

THE POWER OF SELF-CONFIDENCE AND PERSONAL IMAGE

Self-confidence is like a superpower.
Once you start to believe in yourself, magic starts to happen.
—Oscar Auliq-Ice

I received an email today from a high-ranking executive in the government. He wrote, "I am flirting with the idea of having you literally curate my wardrobe. I have many clothes but don't like how I look in them."

This may be the most common complaint I hear from new clients. There's nothing worse than looking in the mirror and not liking what you see. I know this feeling firsthand and experienced it for much of my life. I used to spend countless hours in front of my closet, grappling with what to wear, feeling increasingly frustrated as rejected clothes piled up on the floor. Whether it was a job interview, a presentation, or a date, the pressure to look perfect only heightened my anxiety.

One particularly memorable occasion was my friend Terri's wedding. I was going solo and a man I had dated would be there, so I aimed to look good and maybe even turn heads. As I sifted through my wardrobe, the clock ticking mercilessly, I realized I was about to miss the ceremony altogether.

Sitting amidst the discarded garments, feeling utterly defeated, I received an unexpected call from my mom. Her unconventional advice that it was okay to go to the reception caught me off guard. But it motivated me to do just that. I hastily threw together an outfit—simple yet flattering—and rushed to the reception, determined not to let my wardrobe woes ruin the day. Little did I know this decision would alter the course of my life.

As fate would have it, Jack, the man I had once dated, was also attending solo. Our chance encounter ignited a spark, leading to a reconnection and marriage. It's surreal to think that my inability to choose an outfit nearly cost me the love of my life—the father of my child.

Years later, after becoming an image consultant, I learned I wasn't alone. Many people leave their homes uncomfortable in their skin, beating themselves up for how they look, buying clothes they never wear, and wasting time in their closets trying to pull it all together.

The Dove Foundation discovered that this is, in fact, an epidemic. In their Real Truth About Beauty campaign, launched in 2004 and revisited in 2010, they interviewed thousands of women across ten countries and discovered that only 4% considered themselves beautiful.[1] Astounding.

What about men? I had heard men were more confident than women, and this was a gender-specific issue. However, I have learned this isn't the case. According to the National Institutes of Health, many men struggle with physical attractiveness and self-confidence.[2]

Confidence is a complex trait influenced by many factors, including personality, upbringing, cultural norms, and life experience. Self-esteem comes from the inside out. It means you are not dependent upon anyone else to make you feel good about yourself because you already know you are fine just the way you are. You are confident and aware of your strengths and abilities. This is an inherent right. We all deserve to feel self-assured and confident. The fact that too many people of all ages, races, and socioeconomic backgrounds struggle with self-confidence is a sad reality.

In business, self-confidence is a foundational requirement for success, from asking for funding, setting pricing, and hiring the right team to promoting yourself, your business, and your products and services. At work, people who don't believe in their worth don't effectively promote themselves and their ideas; they speak up less often and avoid necessary self-promotion. These issues occur in the corporate world as well as for small business owners and entrepreneurs.

At home, low self-confidence hurts interpersonal relationships, especially regarding trust and intimacy, affecting one's ability to have deep connections in marriage and all meaningful relationships.

I'm not proposing that loving how you look will solve all of these issues, but I will contend that it is the easiest thing you can do to improve your self-esteem. No matter how much self-confidence you possess, I bet you can think of a time you got a new haircut or bought new clothes that made you feel like a million bucks. How you felt about your appearance gave you an emotional boost when you looked in the mirror, which was amplified when you left your house and got compliments from others.

What about when you were asked to wear a uniform and immediately felt like a "different" person? Uniforms can have positive and negative effects. We can feel less responsible for our actions when we dress like everybody else. Conversely, professionals, such as doctors, nurses, judges, police officers, and priests, gain confidence simply by wearing a uniform. For some, merely dressing in business attire for a sales meeting, presentation, or job interview can give them the confidence to perform.

The point is that clothes alter your mood, affecting everything from how you speak to yourself to how you treat your loved ones and coworkers. They also affect how motivated you are to take on new challenges and how good (or bad) you feel about your life.

Hajo Adam and Adam D. Galinsky, Northwestern University professors and researchers, discovered that feeling great about your appearance ignites a chain reaction that allows you to be great. They called it Enclothed Cognition. Their research studied the psychological effects of clothing choices on mindset and performance. They did an experiment where college students were asked to perform a complicated task: some in a doctor's white coat, some in no coat, and some in the same white coat but they were told it was a painter's jacket. The results of the study were remarkable. When students wore the "doctor's coat," they made 50% fewer errors on the same set of tasks than the students in plain clothes or the "painter's jacket." The research proved that you can shift your self-image, mood, and abilities simply by changing the clothes you wear.[3]

In a similar study, university professor Karen Pine wanted to know whether heroic clothing could unconsciously affect students' thought processes. She found what she suspected to be correct. Her experiment showed that simply wearing a Superman T-shirt boosted students' impressions of themselves *and* made them believe they were physically stronger than the control groups.[4]

It sounds hard to believe, but I bet you have experienced this. Can you remember a time you felt great about how you looked? Do you remember carrying that feeling with you throughout the day? Did you hold your head a bit higher or have more skip to your step? Did you speak up more often, set better personal boundaries, and demand to be treated with respect? Maybe this was when you had the confidence to ask for a promotion, a raise, or a date. In psychology, it is widely believed we feel more confident and assertive when we wear formal clothing, more open and agreeable when we wear casual outfits, healthier when we wear exercise clothes, and happier when we wear brighter colors. Try it on and see how you feel.

In the book *Mind What You Wear: The Psychology of Fashion*, Professor Karen J. Pine wrote, "When we asked over 400 people to choose their top reasons for dressing up, this is what they told us:

- To feel confident (73%)
- To be comfortable (52%)
- To express myself (40%)
- To look fashionable (28%)

The Power of Self-Confidence and Personal Image

- To look professional (27%)
- To get noticed (18%)
- To look sexy (14%)
- To show off my body (13%)
- To disguise my body (11%)
- To blend into the background (7%)[5]

The top three are particularly noteworthy: feeling confident, being comfortable in your skin, and expressing yourself are the most critical factors in creating a compelling image and style.

I have been my own case study, witnessing how my self-esteem blossomed as I learned to love how I look. I have seen it in hundreds of other women and men. If you struggle with looking in the mirror and loving what you see, the following pages will give you the instructions you need to leave that behind.

Chapter 2

HOW YOUR APPEARANCE SHAPES OTHERS' OPINIONS

*Clothes are to us as fur and feathers are to beasts and birds;
they not only add to our appearance, but they are our appearance.
How we look to others entirely depends upon what we wear and how we wear it.
Manners and speech are noted afterward and character last of all.*

—Emily Post

One day, a colleague told me about a friend from her local chapter of the National Speakers Association, a funny, articulate, inspirational speaker who had recently done a TEDx Talk, yet he lacked self-confidence. He was recently divorced and ready to reenter the dating scene. The only issue is that John is blind, making it difficult to see how he looks to himself and others.

When we started working together, John couldn't tell that most of his clothes were discolored, torn, stained, and too big for his body. I understood how this would make anyone self-conscious and reluctant to put themselves out there socially or professionally.

I took him through my typical process: We defined how he wanted people on the dating sites to see him, determined his colors, and selected the best clothing styles to fit his physique. He discovered how it *felt* when clothes fit him properly, and we shopped for "looks" that upgraded his appearance. He soon learned to use the world as his mirror, and its feedback was tremendous, boosting his self-confidence and drawing *lots* of attention from dating sites.

Figure 2.0

Using the world as our mirror is beneficial for all of us. Trusting how other people react to us gives us needed information about ourselves. It's similar to crowdsourced feedback that businesses use today to leverage external opinions, feedback, and expert advice. Why not give it a try? If you are unsure how you look, try it on for size; request and observe feedback from others.

I recently read and enjoyed Seth Stephens-Davidowitz's book *Don't Trust Your Gut: Using Data to Get What You Really Want in Life*. It was full of insights and stories that shook my beliefs and opinions on many topics. For example, do you believe opposites attract? He shares a study by Emma Pierson, a computer and data scientist. She studied one million matches on eHarmony, and it turns out this is a myth. Her conclusion: "We are so interested in similarity that we really want to date ourselves."[1]

Don't Trust Your Gut includes many interesting facts on all aspects of life, especially things that aren't obvious or commonly believed. So when

How Your Appearance Shapes Others' Opinions

Stephens-Davidowitz got into his research on misconceptions about how we look and how it matters, I sat up in attention. He shared that facial science discovered two critical things about appearance: "First, and this is deeply depressing, how we look massively influences how far we advance in life. Our appearance has far more of an impact than many of us realize. Second, and this is encouraging, we can greatly improve how we look. In fact, we can improve our appearance far more than many of us realize."[2]

His book also shared research conducted by University of Chicago professor Alexander Todorov, showing the impact of appearance on American voters. As much as we would like to believe we live in a world of meritocracy, it is often not the case and, most notably, does not drive elections. The candidate's appearance is often more important than their policies or performance record.[3] Unfortunately, this is not only true in politics but everywhere, from the business world to the military.

Inspired by the data on appearances, Seth Stephens-Davidowitz shared in his book about his own study. He learned something I have observed in myself and my clients: we are not accurate judges of how we come across to others. Too many biases get in the way of seeing ourselves clearly. Stephens-Davidowitz wanted to go deeper into this for his own life. He was specifically interested in how competent *he* looked to others. He uploaded a selfie in FaceApp, an app that uses artificial intelligence to alter your photo. It can retouch your appearance to make you look like a movie star, and illustrate how you look as an older or younger version of yourself, and you can test changes to your looks. For example, if you want to see how you look in glasses, with facial hair, or with a change in hair color or cut, the AI makes these changes.

Stephens-Davidowitz experimented with various looks and put them out for feedback using various social media platforms. He learned something he wasn't expecting. Others saw him as significantly more competent with a beard and glasses, and his smile, which he deemed a flaw, wasn't a factor in the results. His conclusion: "the research is overwhelming that our appearance matters, that we can improve our appearance, and that we are poor judges of our own appearance."[4]

Maybe my client John was on to something. Using the world as our mirror provides us with necessary information. The truth is that impressions, judgments, prejudices, and personal preferences all work beneath our mental radar, leaving us painfully unaware of how the world experiences us.

I have seen this in many of my clients. They are stuck with preconceptions about how they look, both positive and negative, and are often resistant to change. This is why I always prefer teaching in group workshops where the participants get my trained eye and the opinion of others—the viewpoint of people with no vested interest one way or the other, people who tell one another, with kindness, what they see.

If you've watched the wildly popular series *What Not to Wear* on TLC, you have witnessed extreme makeover stories and the associated resistance to change in each episode. The results of these types of makeovers are astounding. They change lives. Why? Because we humans judge one another, and fast. It sounds unkind, and you may say, "Oh, I don't do that. I can look past a person's appearance to see who they are on the inside." We all want to believe that is who we are, but the truth is otherwise. We are hardwired to judge one another based on appearance. It was imperative for our survival. We needed to determine if a friend or foe was approaching us and if we should move toward that person or run for our lives. That survival instinct is built into our DNA and exhibited from birth.

An experiment conducted by Alan Slater, a psychology researcher at the University of Exeter, found that infants pay more attention to attractive adults.[5] More astounding, a researcher at the University of Alberta has shown that parents are more likely to give better care and pay closer attention to good-looking children than unattractive ones.[6]

These researchers concluded that how we look matters dramatically and that beauty is not in the eye of the beholder. What we deem beautiful is innate, an instinct we are born with. Psychologists call it the "halo effect," a cognitive bias that occurs when we experience one trait and assume other positive characteristics, without evidence. For example, attractive individuals are more intelligent, friendly, and competent. The halo effect has been known to influence judgments in professional and academic settings as well as social interactions.[7] It can also affect your income, referred to commonly as the "beauty premium," the income gap between attractive and unattractive people.

Good-looking people have an unfair advantage in all aspects of life. The good news is that while some of this is biological, much of it can be influenced by how we dress and groom ourselves.

One thing is for sure: these judgments occur rapidly. Professors Alexander Todorov and Janine Willis's research found we can judge another's trustworthiness in a tenth of a second.[8] Another study by the University of Toronto discovered that students could decide in as few as five seconds whether a person is charismatic.[9]

How do you feel about designer clothes? A Dutch study found that people wearing name-brand clothes were seen as having higher status than individuals wearing non-designer clothes. What made this especially interesting was that "Perceptions did not differ on any of the other dimensions that might affect the outcome of social interactions. There were no differences in perceived attractiveness, kindness, and trustworthiness." Just status.[10]

In another study, participants looked at photos of men in tailored versus off-the-rack suits for just five seconds. They learned that if you want to look successful, you should get your suit tailored and that men who wear more formal clothing than their casually dressed counterparts are considered more successful and likely to earn more money.[11]

Men, do you want to be seen as more dominant? Just shave your head. A UPenn study found that "men with shaved heads were rated as more dominant than similar men with full heads of hair" and that "men whose hair was digitally removed were perceived as more dominant, taller, and stronger than their authentic selves."[12] This may explain why there is a real movement for men choosing a bald head, especially when losing hair. No longer do they need to worry about the unfortunate comb-over or toupee.

All of this validates my point that what we wear and how we look matter, and first impressions happen surprisingly quickly. The brain "thin-slices"—makes rapid inferences—within a split-second. It turns out our brains only take a fraction of a second to judge certain traits, such as trustworthiness, status, and success.

How long do these first impressions last? That data is equally startling. First impressions and associated biases tend to last and are incredibly difficult to challenge. Research has found that it can take up to six months of regular contact with someone to change their initial impression and alter the lens through which they see you. Why? The brain mechanisms involved in first impressions are closely associated with the limbic system, which regulates emotions.[13] In short, we hate to be wrong. Admitting we made a mistake about the person we call our best friend, someone we hired, or worse yet, someone we started dating is not easy for most of us. The data suggests that the first impression will prevail and persist, regardless of how often new experiences and evidence contradict its accuracy.

To summarize, first impressions happen in a heartbeat and stick like glue. How we appear can impact our success both personally and professionally. People judge us not because they are harsh and shallow but because they were born to do so. Once they decide who they think we are, it likely will stay the same even with new information. And if you see that person infrequently, it can take even longer.

This is vital information because we can use it to our benefit once we understand it. I call it creating an *intentional image*, deciding how we want the world to see us. For most of us, it is simply a matter of expressing visually who we are authentically. After all, it's much harder to pretend to be someone we are not.

Chapter 3

THE ESSENCE OF PERSONAL BRANDING AND STYLE

An authentic and honest brand narrative is fundamental today; otherwise, you will simply be edited out.

—Marco Bizzarri, Gucci, CEO

In an episode of the classic sitcom *Seinfeld*, George comes into the apartment wearing a pair of sweatpants and Jerry responds, "You know the message you're sending out to the world with these sweatpants? You're telling the world, 'I give up. I can't compete in normal society. I'm miserable, so I might as well be comfortable.'"[1]

If that's what the sweatpants said to Jerry, what did they say to George? Could they be subtly sending him the message that he isn't worth it? It's possible that what you wear is what you become. As the *Seinfeld* skit pointed out, it represents who you are.

Wearing sweats around town is not your best look, no matter who you are. However, representing who you are in clothes is much more elusive. You can be highly expressive or more subtle in your approach to expressing who you are visually. In this chapter, we explore exactly what it means to dress your brand. How do we communicate who we are by the way we look?

Consider Serena Williams. I love the game of tennis, and I'm a fan of Serena (and Venus) Williams for the obstacles they overcame and their excellence on the court. Serena recently concluded her professional tennis career and is finally receiving the praise and recognition she deserves. She is among the greatest tennis players of all time. Yet throughout her career, Serena experienced discrimination and disdain from fans, colleagues, and referees. When she entered the scene, the sport almost solely consisted of attractive blondes with slim bodies from affluent families. Serena is Black with a strong, muscular body and an on-court grunt. Unlike her competitors, who learned to play tennis on beautifully manicured courts at country clubs, she and her sister Venus used public courts in the housing projects of Watts and Compton, California.

She was simply too Black, too strong, too poor, and too expressive to fit in.

In an interview, she said, "If people were going to be looking and judging, I might as well use that attention to not only advance as a player but to change the playing field for everyone."[2] She decided her racket was one way to do that. Fashion was another. She smashed barriers of race, age, and background and disrupted traditional customs of dress codes on the tennis court, showing the world what it means to dress your brand boldly and expressively.

Serena started by experimenting with fashion trends, denim, studs, snakeskin, mesh, and other runway trends onto the court. As time went on, however, her on-court fashion evolved beyond style and expression alone. As Tania Flynn, former vice president of apparel design at Nike, described it, "it became about being a woman of power…about the message" Williams conveyed through her clothes, embracing her roles as an activist and mother. Serena's fashion grew to reflect her stance on social issues and her dedication to inspiring change and exclusivity, making each look both a personal statement and a cultural milestone.[3]

Another one of my favorites was the tennis great Andre Agassi. His brand was "the bad boy of tennis." In his book *Open*, he wrote about Wimbledon and why he boycotted playing there for three years: "I resent

The Essence of Personal Branding and Style

rules, but especially arbitrary rules. Why must I wear white? I don't want to wear white. Why should it matter to these people what I wear?" His preferred style, which illustrated his rebellion against the status quo, included a mullet hairstyle, jeans, shorts, and neon.[4] Like Serena, Agassi grew up poor and entered the sport of tennis with only a high school diploma. He didn't fit in with his wealthier, more highly educated counterparts, nor did he want to.

You likely aren't in a situation where you are on an international stage with a bone to pick with the social norms. But you may be different in overt or subtle ways and choose to wear that difference like a badge of honor. I was recently in London on vacation and found myself amidst a transgender pride parade. I had a similar experience in Berlin the previous summer: a large gay pride parade. In both cases, these individuals had a different dress code than the masses. If I had jumped into the parade, sporting my American tourist apparel, I would have been the one out of place. They wore outlandish colors and highly provocative styles in leather, mesh, and metal fabrics. Their hair was cut in wild styles in pink, blue, purple, and other vibrant colors. They had tattoos and piercings. They were dressing the part, dressing to communicate something they stood for that was a bit on the fringes, and they were proud to do so.

In business, politics, and more mainstream activities, even for those on center stage, the statement commonly made with one's choice of clothing and appearance is more nuanced.

In November 2020, when Vice President Kamala Harris stepped on stage with President Biden to deliver acceptance speeches, she felt the moment's importance. She represented the hopes and dreams of so many. How do you dress for such an occasion? Indeed, she wore nothing we had seen her wear previously. She made a statement in her white pantsuit and white silk pussy-bow blouse—garments that have been symbols of women's rights for decades and had recently taken on even more meaning. When the world watched that night, her wardrobe was not about fashion. It was politics.

YOUR ULTIMATE STYLE BLUEPRINT

What about Joe Biden? The most significant statement was likely his blue tie, representing his political party and some believed a future of hope—blue skies to come. Presidents have always used clothing as part of their political toolbox. John F. Kennedy distinguished himself from the previous generation by opting for single-breasted suits instead of the more formal double-breasted styles favored by Roosevelt and Truman. Barack Obama did the same by often abandoning the tie altogether. George W. Bush wore cowboy boots, and Donald Trump wore long red ties.

For most of us, our brand and associated personal style are much more subtle. We simply strive to feel beautiful or handsome in a way that communicates who we are. That might be smart, creative, innovative, sophisticated, modern, trendy, bold, feminine, suave—anything you choose. It is about showing up professionally to be seen and heard, viewed as a leader or an expert in your field. This gets to the heart of creating a personal brand.

When teaching or speaking to a group, I often start by asking, "What is a personal brand, and do you have one?" I commonly receive comments like, "Yes, I'm a financial advisor," "I always wear pearls," or " I wear black from head to toe—that's my brand."

I politely explain that a personal brand is deeper. It's who you are on the inside, a reflection of your values. Whether you are a financial advisor, doctor, attorney, realtor, entrepreneur, mom, or dad, these are roles you play in your life. They are what you do, not who you are. If you always wear pearls, black, or a blue blazer, this is how you dress. It is not your brand. Once you have a brand, you may choose these items to express it in the same way you might decorate your home to be modern, country, or colonial.

To my question "Do you have a personal brand?" the answer is always yes. Everyone has one. Taylor Swift is often quoted as saying, "Your brand is what people say about you when you are not in the room," though the specific source is unclear. We leave a footprint not only in how we look but also in how we behave. A study conducted in the early seventies by Professor Albert Mehrabian at UCLA was the source of what is commonly referred to as the 7-38-55 rule. It indicates that 55% of communication is based on our appearance (including body language), 38% on the tone of our voice, and only 7% on the content of our words.[5] People judge us based on how we look, sound, and behave. At a basic level, this is your brand. Think about the people you know:

- Do you have friends and colleagues you can always rely on, knowing they will return your call, email, or text promptly and help you if you are in need? They are showing you they are reliable.
- What about the friends who send you cards on special occasions, check in on you when you are feeling down or not well, and always have a kind word? They are caring.
- What about someone you know who is brilliant, someone you count on for words of wisdom? Do they prioritize education and demonstrate intellectual curiosity?
- Who do you know who always does the right thing? Who is benevolent and gives back during the holidays, donating time and money for a noble cause?
- Do you know spiritual people who attend church every Sunday, post scripture on social media, and quietly pray before every meal?
- What about someone artistic and crafty?
- Do you know someone who is authentic and tells it like it is?
- Do you have an athletic or health-oriented friend who always eats nutritiously, exercises, and meditates?

I can paint a picture of the people in your life who make a positive impact and how they do it. Those are the behaviors that make up a personal brand. They are not usually intentional. Most people do not say this is who I am or how I want to be perceived by the world, and then go about communicating that. It's typically the other way around. But why not? This is precisely what businesses do. Pause for a minute and think about your favorite companies. What are their values? Are they innovative, customer-oriented, affordable, unique, prestigious? I can guarantee they decided in advance and then created a brand identity to match whatever they chose their business would stand for.

A study in the summer of 2022 found these to be the most loved brands in America:

1. Jimmy Choo
2. Downy
3. Dolce & Gabbana
4. Estée Lauder
5. Oral-B
6. Mercedes-Benz
7. KitKat
8. Nespresso
9. Adidas
10. HelloFresh[6]

Are your favorites on the list? Do your values resonate with theirs? These companies have well-defined and documented brands, and they express their messaging in the colors they use, their logo, their customer service policies, their product packaging, pricing, and everything they do and say. It is evident in their office space, personnel, and policies.

So, what about you? What is your brand image? In the next chapter, that is precisely what you will discover.

Chapter 1

DEFINING YOUR BRAND IDENTITY

Be yourself; everyone else is already taken.
—Oscar Wilde

I recently witnessed my son, Steven, undergo the college application process. If you went through this yourself or have kids who have done so, you know the rigor involved. Rightfully so, colleges are focused on filling their first-year class with a wide variety of students who will complement one another and create an ideal student body. Therefore, they want to learn how each student performs academically and who is behind the application. Thus the college essay—tell us who you are, in 650 words or less—is a challenge for high school seniors, as it would be for most adults.

How do you convey who you are as a person in a page and a half? Yet I am amazed at how creatively and brilliantly these young people do exactly that. They artfully communicate who they are. They express their personal brand.

I challenge you to write an imaginary college essay. Share it with trusted friends and family for feedback. Ask yourself who you are and what differentiates you from others. If you were to be part of a fictitious student body of peers and people who surround you personally and professionally, what would you want them to know about you? Once done, consider narrowing it to a few sentences or even adjectives.

Alternatively, try a personal mission statement instead of a college essay. Consider modeling it after companies with impressive mission statements, a short statement of why an organization exists and how it wants to be positioned in the marketplace. When I resonate with a company's mission and identify with its core values, I feel connected to it and am more inclined to buy its products or services. It is like knowing a person's values and deciding if you want to spend more time with them.

CORPORATE EXAMPLES

Bert and John Jacobs, the founders of Life is Good, were part of a panel of CEOs at a conference I attended years ago. What they said on that stage resonated with me, yet there were others on that platform I can barely remember. If you visit the Life is Good website (www.lifeisgood.com), you will see their mission: "Spreading the Power of Optimism. Life isn't Easy. Life isn't Perfect. Life is Good." On the stage that day they also stated, "Each one of us has a choice: to focus our energy on obstacles or opportunities, to fixate on our problems or focus on solutions. We can harp on what is wrong with the world (see most news media), or we can cultivate what's right with the world. What we focus on grows. That is why the Life is Good community shares one simple, unifying mission: to spread the power of optimism. Optimism is not irrational cheerfulness or 'blind' positivity. It is a pragmatic strategy for approaching life. Optimism empowers us to explore the world with open arms and an eye toward solutions, progress, and growth. It also makes life a hell of a lot more fun."[1] They simply sell merchandise. It's their mission and messaging that is inspiring.

Are you familiar with Warby Parker (www.warbyparker.com)? They have revolutionized how we buy eyewear. College students Neil

Defining Your Brand Identity

Blumenthal, David Gilboa, Jeffrey Raider, and Andrew Hunt, the co-founders, were frustrated with the high cost of eyewear under a single-provider system. Their mission: "To inspire and impact the world with vision, purpose, and style. We aim to demonstrate that a business can scale, become profitable, and do good in the world—without charging a premium for it."[2] Simple yet focused, the Warby Parker mission tells us what they are all about. You will see their brand in motion if you visit them online or at one of their stores. Not only are their glasses beautifully designed, but they are also affordable and the company donates a pair to someone in need for each purchased pair of glasses. Pretty compelling. The Warby Parker website states, "Since day one, over 15 million pairs of glasses have been distributed through our Buy a Pair, Give a Pair program. Alleviating the problem of impaired vision is at the heart of what we do, and with your help, our impact continues to expand."[2] Does this simple statement and brand focus make you want to buy your glasses from Warby Parker? It is the first place I recommend to my clients looking to purchase eyewear.

What about American Express (www.americanexpress.com)? Does their mission affect how you feel about them as a company? "Our mission is to "Become essential to our customers by providing differentiated products and services to help them achieve their aspirations." Additionally, their company values express a focus on customer service, innovation, integrity, diversity and inclusion, open-mindedness, and teamwork. Does their commitment to their employees and customers influence your desire to get and use an American Express credit card?"[3]

Finally, one of my favorite brands is Nordstrom. I appreciate their quality and excellent customer service. Their mission statement is "We exist to help our customers feel good and look their best. Since starting as a shoe store in 1901, how to best serve customers has been central to every decision we make."[4] I shop there regularly for myself and with clients. They live their brand. The personnel is always helpful and looking to satisfy their customers. They make it easy for me to help my clients by setting us up in beautiful dressing rooms and running down sizes. But what I appreciate most is their return policy. If anything goes wrong with anything you purchase, they will take it back, no questions asked. One of my clients bought a pair of shoes positioned as comfortable. After trying and wearing the shoes for six months she was very dissatisfied, and she was able to return her worn shoes for a full refund!

DEVELOPING A PERSONAL BRAND

A personal brand is the same thing—just personal. Consider some famous individuals and their personal mission statements:

> Mahatma Gandhi: "I shall not fear anyone on Earth. I shall fear only God. I shall not bear ill will toward anyone. I shall not submit to injustice from anyone. I shall conquer untruth by truth. And in resisting untruth, I shall put up with all suffering."[5]
>
> Walt Disney's mission was simple: to create joy and happiness for people of all ages. In his own words, "it was all started by a mouse...and that this mouse brought happiness to millions."[6]
>
> Maya Angelou: "My mission in life is not only to survive but to thrive and to do so with some passion, some compassion, some humor, and some style."[7]

It's your turn. Can you quickly and concisely articulate who you are and what you stand for? Ask yourself what matters to you most. What are your values, goals, dreams, and aspirations? You are truly unique. We all have superpowers, things we do better than anyone else. You could be creative, intelligent, funny, thoughtful, inspirational, kind, or empathetic. You may have overcome a significant hurdle, making you an expert due to that experience. Are you able to take complicated concepts and distill them into simple concepts? Do you have grit and tenacity and success because you work harder than everyone else?

Some people who know me well tell me I am too sensitive. Or when they want to be kinder, I am just more sensitive than others. The truth is I do feel things more than others. I am compassionate and feel more pain and disappointment than most people. In my youth, I struggled to change this trait. But today, I know it is my strength. Not only do I get to feel a broader range of emotions, but I also feel other people's ups and downs, making me highly empathetic. Empathy is one of my superpowers. Do you have a trait you wish you didn't have, but if you look at the flip side, you see it is a talent in disguise?

I challenge you to write your "college essay" or personal mission statement. Have fun with it. Share it with trusted friends and colleagues. Save it and reflect on it from time to time. Once that is done, you should get clearer on the image you want to possess and project to the world. Boil your brand down to a small set of adjectives you can keep as a mantra. Figure 4.0 provides a list of adjectives that might help you with the process. Don't feel limited to these words if you have others you think better describe you.

YOUR ULTIMATE STYLE BLUEPRINT

ADJECTIVES

- **A.** Accepting
  - Approachable
  - Artistic
  - Athletic
  - Authentic
- **B.** Beautiful
  - Benevolent
  - Bold
  - Brave
  - Brilliant
- **C.** Caring
  - Casual
  - Charismatic
  - Charming
  - Chic
  - Classic
  - Clever
  - Conservative
  - Confident
  - Consistent
  - Competent
  - Creative
  - Curious
  - Current
- **D.** Daring
  - Detail Oriented
  - Dramatic
- **E.** Edgy
  - Educated
  - Elegant
  - Engaging
  - Enthusiastic
  - Ethical
  - Exciting
  - Expert
- **F.** Feminine
  - Formal
  - Friendly
  - Fun
- **G.** Genuine
  - Generous
- **H.** Handsome
  - Hardworking
  - Hip
  - Honest
- **I.** Important
  - Independent
  - Informed
  - Innovative
  - Inspiring
  - Intelligent
  - Interesting
  - Intriguing
- **K.** Kind
  - Knowledgeable
- **L.** Lively
  - Lovely
  - Loyal
- **M.** Masculine
  - Modern
- **O.** Open-Minded
  - Optimistic
- **P.** Predictable
  - Political
  - Proper
  - Progressive
- **R.** Refined
  - Relevant
  - Reliable
  - Regal
  - Responsive
  - Responsible
- **S.** Savvy
  - Serious
  - Sexy
  - Smart
  - Sophisticated
  - Spiritual
  - Spontaneous
  - Sporty
  - Spunky
  - Stately
  - Strategic
  - Stylish
  - Suave
- **T.** Theatrical
  - Trendy
  - Trustworthy
- **W.** Warm
  - Whimsical
  - Wise
  - Worldly
- **Y.** Youthful

Figure 4.0

Defining Your Brand Identity

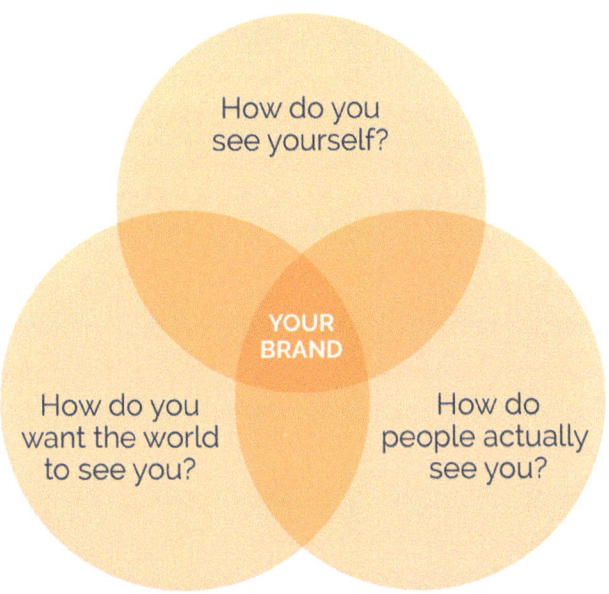

Figure 4.1

When I describe the personal branding process with my clients, I often refer to the graphic shown in Figure 4.1.

Your brand is the intersection of these bubbles. Some people need clarification about the statement of who you are, as compared to how you want others to see you. For many, there is no difference. But there are circumstances where they differ. For example, if you are going through a life transition, were fired from a job, or were recently divorced, you may not feel as confident as you would otherwise. You may want to be a leader but have yet to step into that role emotionally. You may have gained weight and don't feel as attractive as you once did. You also may be changing careers. For example, you may have been an attorney and are now moving into an artistic field. In these cases, you may want others to see you in a way you don't currently see yourself. That's okay. I recommend focusing on how you want others to see you in these cases. Fake it until you become it; show up as the person you want to be, and eventually you will start to believe it.

Next, you will want to consider how others see you, which can be challenging to get one's arms around. People are reluctant to give us direct feedback on the image we project: good, fantastic, bad, or ugly. However, discovering this information is critical for success.

When I work privately with clients, I help them acquire this feedback through an anonymous survey. I recommend you do this yourself. It can be challenging to hear this type of feedback, but if you take what you hear constructively, it can be powerful. Most of what you will hear will be heartwarming and complimentary. But you may, for example, learn that people find you unapproachable or intimidating. If that's the case, it's common and easily fixed.

I had a lovely client, yet the problem was that she wanted to be something other than lovely. She was gracious and kind but wanted to be seen as modern and a bit edgy. So we worked on how she could dress and even behave in ways that weren't unkind or rude but also not overly sweet and demure so that she could change this perception. We had to start by understanding what she wanted and comparing that to how others experienced her.

Getting this feedback is a simple process. Below is an example format that you can tweak and make your own. I recommend you use an application such as Google Forms. Set up the survey to be anonymous. Ask questions to get the answers you desire. About 50% of the individuals who agree to complete the survey actually will. Therefore, the larger your list of invitees, the better. Consider thirty people as a minimum so you have at least a fifteen-person sample size.

My process works like this:

- Send an email to your list explaining that you are in the process of creating an authentic personal brand and that you would like their help. I refer to mine as a 360-degree survey because it is best to include the people surrounding you—family, employees, supervisors, clients, friends, acquaintances, and so on.

Defining Your Brand Identity

- Send them the survey, give them a deadline, and remind them that you want honest feedback, that it is anonymous, and that the form is set up so you cannot tell who sent the response. You will likely need to follow up with them multiple times; people get busy, so you want a commitment up front.
- Consider closing the loop after receiving feedback to let them know what you learned about yourself and how you will implement that into your life and brand.

In the survey, ask questions that will help you. I typically include these:

- **Question 1:** Please choose fewer than five adjectives to describe [your name]. (List a bunch of adjectives, the ones you want them to pick and many you don't. I put them in alphabetical order to help disguise the preferred options.)
- **Question 2:** Do you know [your name] personally, professionally, or both? (This can help you understand how your brand plays out in different aspects of your life.)
- **Question 3:** If you know [your name] both personally and professionally, would you use different words to describe them in different settings?
- **Question 4**: If you answered Yes above, please explain here:
- **Question 5:** What do you MOST value about [your name]?
- **Question 6**: What do you LEAST value about [your name]?
- **Question 7:** What one thing should [your name] KEEP doing?
- **Question 8:** What one thing should [your name] STOP doing?
- **Question 9:** Can you think of any attitudes, traits, behaviors, or anything about how [your name] shows up in the world that might be getting in their way of success?

As I mentioned above, putting yourself out there like this takes courage. Not all of my private clients choose to do it. Some don't want to risk hurtful feedback. For this reason, consider a large enough sample size that one individual who may be jealous or competitive with you shows up as an outlier. Look for trends and don't get stuck on feedback from one person. If you get negative responses, I recommend you take in the feedback and ask yourself, "Is that true about me?" You know yourself.

Information is power. Understanding how others see you can be vitally important to being your best.

Ultimately, you will want to compare the brand you have chosen for yourself to the feedback from others. This can be wonderfully empowering. You will likely learn many flattering things people feel about you. If there are a few things you were hoping people would say that they didn't, you will primarily focus on that as you do the next step: learning to express your brand through your appearance.

Are you wondering about having multiple brands to support different aspects of your life? If so, this is a common question, and the answer is nuanced. Mostly, you are the same person whether at work, on a date, with friends, with your kids, at church, or elsewhere. Therefore, one set of adjectives and one brand identity should be the goal. However, if you want to be sexy on a date, not at work or with your friends and family, that could be an exception, or perhaps you're seeking a promotion and want to be taken more seriously at work but not at home. You may adapt your appearance for a specific setting and purpose. But in general, you are who you are, and showing up authentically is easier and more fulfilling.

Joan (not her real name) was a serious litigation attorney working for a "white shoe" law firm in downtown Washington, DC. She described her closet as confused. It was full of black suits, stiff-collared tops, closed-toed shoes, and traditional jewelry—precisely what the judge and her partners needed to see. She also had long, flowing maxi dresses, beads, funky sandals, and some very tasteful yet sexy styles. As Joan went through the process of creating her personal brand, she described herself as feminine, sexy, bohemian, and carefree. She started to see how stressful it was to dress for work in ways that were inconsistent with her values and preferences. As a

Defining Your Brand Identity

fix, we discussed adhering to her professional dress code while still being true to herself. Joan started wearing undergarments that were feminine, sexy, and bohemian. She told me it was surprisingly empowering; she felt like she had a secret under that dark suit where her true self existed.

She now practices law in the not-for-profit space where she can be more visually expressive and consistent with her core values. If you are like Joan and your job dictates a persona different from your innate personality, you may need to adhere to that dress code. This is an exception, and like Joan, you might find, if you are forced to dress and act in ways inconsistent with your authentic self, it might be time for a change.

Chapter 5

ARTFULLY EXPRESSING YOUR PERSONALITY AND VALUES

Style is a way to say who you are without having to speak.
—Rachel Zoe

To create a captivating and individualized style, you need to know what you want to communicate and also envision that style. Once you can see it in your mind's eye, you can build a closet full of clothes you love, a wardrobe that leaves you feeling confident and communicates who you are and how you want to be seen. This will allow you to show up for a client meeting, a job interview, a date, a luncheon, a networking event, a conference, or your kid's soccer match, consistently communicating with intention. The idea is to look in the mirror every time you get dressed and ask yourself if you are communicating your brand through your appearance and if you look the part of someone who is [fill in the blank with your adjectives].

In Chapter 13, I will walk you through a closet audit based on everything you have learned in the book. For now, you can start by going through your clothes and asking yourself if each shirt, jacket, pair of pants, dress, pair of shoes, scarf, tie, piece of jewelry, etc. adheres to your adjectives. Can you label things sophisticated, romantic, dramatic, modern, classic, and so on? To better understand what I mean, see Figure

YOUR ULTIMATE STYLE BLUEPRINT

5.0 for examples of art styles. Can you project these styles onto your wardrobe items?

Creative
"In a Levantine Port"
Artist: John Singer Sargent

Romantic
Artist: Olga Novitskaya

Dramatic
"Atlantic Storm"
Artist: Samuel Earp

Sophisticated
Artist: Steve Johnson

Edgy
"Edgy"
Artist: Vesna Delevska

Whimsical
"Curiosity"
Artist: Cindy Thornton

Modern
"Yellow-Red-Blue"
Artist: Wassily Kandinsky

Figure 5.0

Artfully Expressing Your Personality and Values

Ask yourself if your wardrobe matches your adjectives. If you have decided you are edgy, bold, outspoken, and direct, for example, you will want bright, vibrant, and dramatic clothes. If you have dresses with ruffles, bows, hearts, and sparkles, this does not align with your adjectives. Those are items ordinarily found in the closet of someone who has chosen words like sweet, demure, lovely, and feminine.

Spoiler alert: if you're like most people, you will likely discover you need an overhaul of items that tell your story; this is further exemplified when we go through future chapters and uncover the things that do and don't flatter you physically. You can change your wardrobe to match your new style guidelines as quickly or slowly as you choose. The pressure to make these changes is 100% up to you.

Let's look at the most common adjectives people choose and what types of clothing and accessories match their words.

ACCOMPLISHED

Are you a leader or an aspiring leader? Are C-level executives your ideal clients? If so, you want to be sure others see you as successful and at the top of your game. You will likely want to dress the part of an executive with presence and panache. Your clothing designs and fabrics should communicate quality; the same goes for your jewelry, shoes, and other accessories. It is a mistake for someone who wants to convey success to show up with ill-fitting clothes. Be sure your clothes fit your body perfectly. Plan to use a tailor to alter most items in your closet.

You will want to go to the next level with all your outfits for an accomplished appearance. I refer to this as "finishing" your look. Jackets, scarves, quality accessories, and shoes should be a staple in your wardrobe. If you wear jeans, choose a trouser style and a dark wash. Avoid faded jeans or fad styles.

An accomplished look means you are at home in solids and subtle patterns. This does not mean you are boring. Your clothes are likely designer pieces, making them more exclusive with high craftsmanship. You can add punch to your outfit with a bright-colored shirt, bag, tie, or shoes. An accomplished style is typically not trendy; instead, it consists of timeless pieces, making each item worth the investment. This doesn't mean you must spend more on your wardrobe than other personal styles. You never have to pay retail if you shop at the end of each season, at consignment stores or quality outlets.

APPROACHABLE

I have yet to work with anyone for whom being approachable was unimportant. You may have this trait inherently. If not, you may be shy and introverted; therefore, people may not see you as friendly or warm. You may even have a facade that makes you standoffish or intimidating to others. In this case, you may want to make changes to be seen as approachable—for example, staying clear of a wardrobe of black and gray pieces. Instead, try lighter, softer, happier colors and fabrics. Look for patterns and accessories with curved, soft lines instead of harsh, straight lines—anything that feels fun, warm, or inviting.

Women, ensure you accessorize and consider pearls or bling instead of metal. Choose feminine patterns, like polka dots and paisley designs. Avoid stiff collars, harsh color combinations, and structured prints such as plaids and checks. Men, it would help if you avoided black and gray. Instead, wear navy blue suits with a fun tie or throw in a pink shirt. Add some manly bling and a subtle cologne. Finally, if you want to be approachable, slow down when you enter a room. Be sure you have eye contact and smile at new people you meet. Allow your intentionally approachable image to drape across the room.

Artfully Expressing Your Personality and Values

BOLD, EDGY, DRAMATIC

Do you consider yourself bold, edgy, or dramatic? Do you stand out from the crowd, raise your hand often to be heard, ask provocative questions, or proclaim things others might be too timid to say? Are you fearless in introducing innovative ideas, advocating for change, and saying it like it is? Then you are bold, and how you dress should reflect that style.

If your appearance is inconsistent with your personality, it is psychologically jarring to others. People expect you to act in a way that reflects how you look. So if you are bold, you should wear bright, loud, and unexpected colors, patterns, textures, shoes, eyewear, and accessories. Depending on your profession, you may be able to get away with tattoos or piercings. Your hair and makeup can be untraditional. How much or how little bold and edgy you bring into your image depends on your personality, your lifestyle, and the other adjectives you choose.

I have a client whom I will refer to as Carla. Carla hired me because she was a successful mid-level manager in a high-tech company, but her personality was getting in her way. Her company wanted to promote her to the next level of management, but her reviews indicated that both her team and coworkers found her to be "acrid, abrupt, and too direct." My first impulse was to help her focus on a more approachable style, but when we tried that on for size, she told me she received anecdotal feedback that it backfired. People were finding her more abrupt and off-putting than ever. However, the input improved when we did the opposite and had her dress in bold and dramatic styles. She worked on her soft skills in the office, but we discovered that her direct, sometimes confrontational interpersonal style seemed more pronounced when she wore more subtle clothing. The contrast was too severe. But when she wore dramatic, vibrant colors and patterns, her loud voice and direct manner felt softer in comparison. Carla was brilliant and did move up the ladder at her company. She is now recognized as a go-getter who tells it like it is. She is respected for her innovative ideas, and she challenges others to be their best. It would have been a shame if, instead, her natural personality traits had gotten in the way of all she had to offer her company and stifled her career growth.

CREATIVE, ARTISTIC, INTERESTING, UNIQUE

Many people are creative even if they are not necessarily artsy. You may work in an artistic field: photographer, interior designer, fashion designer, or graphic artist. You might be an out-of-the-box, creative thinker known for developing new ideas or innovating.

When I was a full-time photographer, I found it ironic that the informal uniform of the photography industry is black. This makes sense when capturing the moments of a live event when you want to blend into the background, when you want to be a fly on the wall, observing the party and not bringing attention to yourself. But don't you think a photographer should appear creative? Why would you believe they will deliver a creative product when they look dark and dull? What about interior designers? Should they illustrate that they understand color and design through the clothes, jewelry, shoes, and eyewear they wear? Have you ever hired a hairstylist with dull, boring hair or a makeup artist who does not wear makeup? I hope not. The same subliminal messaging occurs if you are a marketing expert, a writer, or an innovative business leader. People will believe you are interesting if you dress the part.

For a creative style, look for shoes that are different and unique. Buy handmade jewelry from artisans, not items that are mass-manufactured in China. Be aware of brands that others will buy as well. A typical creative will want to be seen as looking different from everyone (or anyone) else. Try various color combinations, shop at boutiques, and find unique brands that others won't have. Consider a creative hairstyle or the addition of a few strands of an accent color. If you like vintage styles, add an item to your outfit. I would caution not to go overboard because you can look like you have a costume on if you do too many things simultaneously. But have fun playing with this idea and trying different looks.

MODERN, HIP, TRENDY

Do you follow fashion trends? Do you like to know what's in style and buy a few or many new pieces each season to be sure you're always in vogue? There are numerous reasons to want to bring a bit of trendiness into your life. You might be hip, a fashionista who buys the hottest styles right off the runway. Or you could be a classic dresser, but you like bringing current items into your wardrobe to look contemporary and relevant. I commonly recommend this for my "clients of a certain age" who want to be sure they are not seen as "has-beens." You may be in technology, politics, medicine, or another field that requires you to be and appear current, that you are in touch with progress, that you know what is going on in the industry and the world.

No matter how much or how little modern, hip, and trendy you want to bring into your look, one thing is for sure: you cannot appear dated. Avoid decade-old hairstyles, clothing, and accessories. You don't have to overhaul your whole wardrobe yearly, but you should bring in a few key pieces. Knowing what is in or out of style is very important to anyone who wants to communicate that they are on the cutting edge or even in touch with the times.

LOVELY, WARM, CHARMING

Are you kind, thoughtful, and soft-spoken? Do people refer to you as quiet, gentle, and warm? Are you a good listener? Do you prioritize thoughtfulness, empathy, and compassion? If these sound like you, if these are some adjectives you would choose, then you want your wardrobe to match these words.

In this case, you will likely feel best in soft fabrics with movement and happy colors that are not too bright. Your hair will likely be soft with some movement, whether male or female. Stiff or harsh materials, saturated colors, contrasting colors like black and white, or dull colors like gray should not be in your wardrobe.

Remember, if you show up in vivid colors with contrasting patterns, people will expect your personality to match. If you prefer to be quieter and not draw much attention to yourself, or if you like to avoid conflict, then lean toward things that feel calmer, peaceful, and Zen-like.

ORGANIZED, RELIABLE, LOYAL

Many individuals in business are known for their organizational skills. They work in companies that prioritize reliability and efficiency. This could include accountants, administrators, individuals in support roles, government employees at all levels, lawyers, doctors, and financial advisors—anyone required to be trustworthy, disciplined, and conscientious.

Years ago, I found it ironic that I hired a recommended professional organizer who had a very disheveled appearance. She was good at what she did, but I saw how her appearance directly and negatively affected her ability to gain clients and earn money. When we meet professionals who make a living by being thorough and systematic, they must present themselves in a neat and orderly manner. They must be punctual and have a structured presence. If not, they unconsciously send a mixed message that can hinder their success. My professional organizer, Paula (not her real name), eventually attended one of my workshops and received this feedback from the group. She completely changed her wardrobe. Not only did she look and feel more attractive and confident, but over time, her business thrived. She noticed more people approaching her at networking events, which converted to sales.

Remember, how you look is your most powerful nonverbal communication tool. Here's another example: Sarah (again, not her real name) is a financial advisor who almost always wore skintight clothes and very high heels. She often posted images of herself on social media in alluring poses in sexy clothing, even a tiny bikini. I am not making a statement on morality. There is a place for this type of dress in one's life, but in this case, it conflicted with her intended image. When we started working together, Sarah picked intelligent, trustworthy, approachable, current, and polished as her adjectives. She was confusing sexy attire with a polished, stylish, put-together appearance. With anonymous feedback, she learned some people didn't take her seriously, and some were critical and potentially felt jealous or threatened by her overt sex appeal. Her appearance overshadowed the fact that she was competent. It was a simple fix to move from a sexy, alluring appearance to one that was stunning yet sophisticated and better matched her objectives and career aspirations. We left a few of her favorite pieces in her wardrobe for those occasions when she wanted to bring a bit of sex appeal into her personal life.

APPLYING STYLE SYSTEMS

These are just a few examples of personal styles based on adjectives. They are not absolutes—the idea is not to paint yourself into a box. You are a complex being with different moods and a varied lifestyle. Whatever your image, just be intentional. There are no mistakes if you are purposeful in your decisions.

For many people, this is easier said than done. It's one thing to decide on the image you want to project. It's another to apply that to your appearance. For this reason, over thirty years ago, Master Stylist Alyce Parsons developed a Universal Style System that has become the gold standard for image consultants. The system created a language for both men and women to see themselves in a style category that helped them dress authentically. The seven universal styles for men and women are:

YOUR ULTIMATE STYLE BLUEPRINT

1. Elegant/Sophisticated
2. Classic/Traditional
3. Sporty/Natural
4. Creative
5. Dramatic/Modern
6. Romantic
7. Sexy/Seductive

As Alyce Parsons shares in her 1990 book *StyleSource: The Power of the Seven Universal Styles for Women and Men,* you can be one or a combination of these styles.[1]

Other systems help people identify a style category and what it means. My first exposure to the style world was through House of Colour out of the United Kingdom.[2] They used a psychological quiz that led to a style category based on fairy-tale figures like an ingénue, fairy godmother, gamine, or queen. These systems help you imagine a character or prototype to follow as you learn to create a consistent look and feel for your style.

In my business, Success thru Style, I created nine female avatars. Each has three different appearances: skin tone, features, and hairstyles. Like Alyce Parsons, my goal was to help my clients—when adjectives were not enough—understand and visualize a character to emulate. One of my clients, Cathy, said that seeing herself as the cute avatar helped her shop and dress when she was not feeling great. Cathy is always beautiful, but I am glad the avatars helped her during this time. The Success thru Style Avatars™ are:

1. Active Anna
2. Classic Claire
3. Sophisticated Sophia
4. Boho Bethany
5. Exotic Eva
6. Feminine Fiona

Artfully Expressing Your Personality and Values

7. Dramatic Darla
8. Chic Cara
9. Creative Cleo

Compared to Parson's Universal Style, I added a few categories and omitted sexy/alluring. After working with hundreds of women, no one has chosen this option. Instead, it is something added for specific occasions. Women can add a little sex appeal by color choice, how taut the fabric is, how high the heel is, or how much skin is shown. The same is true for men: the tautness of their clothes, chest showing, and maybe some jewelry can add a sexy touch to their existing wardrobe. In both cases, a touch of fragrance can send the right signals.

Ladies, take a look at the Success thru Style Avatars™ that follow. Read each description and check out the styles shown in the illustrations. Who do you most relate to?

YOUR ULTIMATE STYLE BLUEPRINT

Figure 5.1

Active Anna (Figure 5.1) is alive, vibrant, and energetic. She is active and may be athletic. Either way, she is likely health-oriented, making time to care for herself inside and out. Her wardrobe is comfortable and easy, yet appealing and well put together. She never wants to be slowed down by her clothing or shoes. Therefore, she prefers flats, platforms, or kitten heels to high heels and wouldn't be caught dead in Spanx or any other binding shapewear. Her accessories are likely minimal, and she prefers a natural face and easy-to-manage hair.

If you are an Active Anna, people probably view you as the go-to person who gets things done—with vim, vigor, and vitality!

Artfully Expressing Your Personality and Values

Figure 5.2

Sophisticated Sophia (Figure 5.2) is refined, polished, and elegant. She exudes self-confidence and rightfully so! She is accomplished and driven. Her wardrobe commands attention with well-made designer clothes. She always completes her look from head to toe with shoes, a matching bag, quality jewelry, and other accessories with attention to detail. Sophia makes time to go to the salon to get her roots highlighted and her nails polished.

If you resonate with Sophisticated Sophia, congratulations are in order. You didn't get there overnight. It takes hard work, conviction, and tenacity to be a style leader whom others admire and emulate.

Figure 5.3

Classic Claire (Figure 5.3) is loyal, conscientious, and responsible. She is understated, not one to bring attention to herself. She prefers a support role to being in the limelight. She chooses timeless clothing, usually in solid and subtle colors—nothing bright or showy. Her accessories and jewelry are simple pieces she can wear daily, which work for most occasions. Claire also goes for a clean, natural look in makeup, and her hairstyle is practical and easy to wear.

If you are like Classic Claire, you are likely a huge comfort to many who know they can rely on you. Your contributions are tremendous and should never be underestimated.

Artfully Expressing Your Personality and Values

Figure 5.4

Feminine Fiona (Figure 5.4) is kind, gracious, nurturing, and romantic. She never wants to insult or harm others. Fiona loves to wear dresses, skirts, and soft fabrics in feminine colors. She enjoys how it feels to be in high heels and doesn't mind that others might find them uncomfortable. Pearls and bling are her go-to choices for accessories. Fiona prefers her hair on the longer side with curls and movement and wouldn't be caught dead without "her face on."

If you resonate with Feminine Fiona, you are happiest helping others. You like being a woman and use your feminine charm in all aspects of your life. It is important to you that others find you approachable and friendly.

YOUR ULTIMATE STYLE BLUEPRINT

 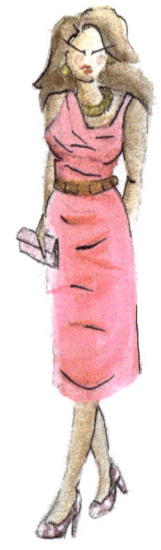 

Figure 5.5

Exotic Eva (Figure 5.5) is worldly, genuine, and exciting. She loves to travel and learn about other cultures and is both adventurous and intriguing to others. Eva can be found in prints, designs, fabrics, and accessories that speak of different cultures. Her jewelry, accessories, and clothing are often unique and handmade, things she found abroad. She loves to express her love of the whole world in her wardrobe. Her hair and makeup are dramatic.

If you are drawn to the style of Exotic Eva, you likely live life fully and courageously and have an unusual sense of adventure that is infectious and stimulating to those around you.

Artfully Expressing Your Personality and Values

Figure 5.6

Dramatic Darla (Figure 5.6) is bold, daring, and a risk-seeking. She is confident in her life and wardrobe and unafraid to draw attention to herself. She loves vibrant colors that make a splash—bold prints and edgy designs are her mainstay. She does not wear girly prints or flowy dresses. She may be a leather-and-metal gal or a little larger than life. Darla's hairstyle, makeup, eyewear, and accessories are statement pieces.

If you see yourself relating to Dramatic Darla, that's good for you. You live in full color. I can only imagine how amazing the world would be if we had more Darlas!

YOUR ULTIMATE STYLE BLUEPRINT

Figure 5.7

Creative Cleo (Figure 5.7) is original, fun, and inventive. She may be artistic or simply an outside-the-box thinker. She has a wardrobe full of things that other people call interesting. Her ideal outfit combines uncommon items. She would be mortified to show up at a party or event and see another woman in the same outfit!! But not to worry; her ingenuity ensures that it will never happen. Cleo might sport a funky, colorful hairstyle; she may have tattoos or piercings; she may enjoy thrift shops where she can find rare treasures that make an outfit.

If you see yourself in Cleo, you are open to new things and may pave the way for women to think and dress outside the box. Keep it up! You inspire many who don't speak up and who hesitate to express who they are.

Artfully Expressing Your Personality and Values

Figure 5.8

Chic Cara (Figure 5.8) is stylish, modern, and trendy. She has no intention of letting her appearance get dated. She loves to shop and considers adding new "finds" to her wardrobe fun and invigorating. Cara follows the trends and likely updates her wardrobe each season. Her hair, nails, and makeup are also in vogue. She prioritizes appearance over comfort and will endure high heels and tight clothing if it suits the outfit.

If you are like Cara, you will seem forever young and never look or feel dated, no matter your age.

YOUR ULTIMATE STYLE BLUEPRINT

Figure 5.9

Boho Bethany (Figure 5.9) is carefree, authentic, and youthful. She is feminine and soft-spoken and doesn't follow the trends. She wears what she likes: clothes with lots of movement and handcrafted items made from beads, stone, leather, and maybe even feathers and crystals. She finds business attire challenging because she thinks most of it is boring. She likes flowy styles that are uniquely her own, expressing her inner hippie and open, optimistic outlook. Bethany is grounded and holistic, preferring natural tones and a low-maintenance style. She likes to be comfortable and is often in sandals and flats. She may wear her hair long and likes to play with makeup.

If you resonate with Bethany, you are likely relaxed and easygoing. You are probably a bit "woo-woo" or "touchy-feely" according to others. You are a comfort to many around you who are stressed and taking life too seriously. Just being in your presence puts other people at ease.

Artfully Expressing Your Personality and Values

You aren't alone if it feels confining to pick just one avatar. Most of us are a combination.

I, for example, am a mix of Creative Cleo, Sophisticated Sophia, and Feminine Fiona. I see myself as creative and strive for originality. I prioritize being compassionate and approachable, yet I want to be seen as a leader in my field, someone who is accomplished and self-assured. What about you?

If you gravitate to one or a few avatars, you may want to check out my Pinterest boards at https://www.pinterest.com/cyndyporter/ where I have a board for each avatar. This will show you items each avatar may have in their closet. If you are a Pinterest user, I recommend you create your own style board. I emphasize the importance of seeing the image you want to create for yourself in your mind's eye. You have likely been buying and wearing the same style of clothing for many years, if not all of your adult life. Since you are reading this book, you have decided to change all of that. If you don't have a solid idea of what you want for your future self, it will only be natural to revert to what you have always done. Envisioning your future self is critical to that goal.

As you consider your ideal future image and style, you may want to look around for someone or a few people you might like to emulate—someone in the political scene, a movie star, a character in a favorite show, or even someone you know personally. Pay attention to other people's appearances. What do you like? What do you dislike? This is a great way to achieve awareness around the style you want and don't want to create for yourself.

Learning to communicate your personality and values visually is powerful. If you take nothing away from this book other than the knowledge to do that, you will be considerably further along than most people. It will guide you in deciding what to buy when you shop. Having a closet full of clothes that are objects of communication is truly transformational. You will see a shift in how people respond to

YOUR ULTIMATE STYLE BLUEPRINT

you, and you will begin to love how you look. But we aren't going to stop here. In the book's next section, we will unravel how to look your personal best. There are eight billion humans on the planet, and no two of us look alike. There will indeed be women who choose the same avatars and men with the same adjectives. For the most part, they don't resemble one another physically. You will learn how to dress your unique body and physical traits to express who you are and enhance your physical attractiveness.

Section II

THE ART OF DRESSING FOR YOUR UNIQUE FEATURES

The human form is the greatest masterpiece of art.
—*Commonly attributed to Michelangelo*

Imagine you are the architect of your own image, designing a structure that reflects your personal brand and style. Just as architecture varies from sleek modern lines to intricate Gothic details, your personal brand can embody different looks. As we have discussed, whether you prefer bold contemporary fashion, timeless classic attire, or unique eclectic trends, your style reflects your identity. In any medium, the fundamental elements of art remain the same. Their application, however, makes each work unique. Similarly, to enhance your unique physical traits, you'll use the principles of art and design: line, shape, proportion, color, texture, scale, and pattern.

Human beings are like unique three-dimensional canvases, each an object of art. Our raw materials include hairstyle color and texture, skin tone, features of various sizes and shapes, and bodies of different forms and proportions. Understanding your features and physical traits—what you love and what you might want to de-emphasize—is fundamental to dressing in a way that presents your best self and makes you love how you look.

If you are analytical, you might like to hear there is a math equation for beauty called the golden mean or the golden ratio, which is written as $\Phi=(1+\sqrt{5})/2$. When this formula is applied to physical objects, such as a human body, face, flower, or seashell, it conforms to what we see as universally appealing (Figure A).[1]

Figure A

The Art of Dressing for Your Unique Features

The ancient Greeks believed there were three ingredients to beauty: symmetry, balance, and harmony. I love this definition, and when we apply art principles to how we look and dress, we keep these three ingredients in mind to achieve our own personal definition of beauty.

Section II of *Your Ultimate Style Blueprint* will guide you in creating and presenting yourself as a work of art leveraging these principles. You will learn how to apply art principles to your physical attributes and the clothes you wear. You will discover how to dress to showcase your best features while camouflaging any perceived flaws. By the end of this section you will know everything you need to create a personal style that is uniquely yours and leaves a lasting impression.

Note that in Section II you will be introduced to many new principles. None are individually complex, but combined there can be much to remember. To help you retain this information, I created a cheat sheet that you can download from my website under the Resources section (https://successthrustyle.com/resources/my-style-blueprint/). Start by completing the first item: a description of your personal brand, including your brand adjectives. You will be reminded to update Your Ultimate Style Blueprint Summary Sheet at various junctures throughout the remaining chapters. When it's complete, consider taking a picture so you can keep this information with you when you dress and shop.

Chapter 6

EMBRACING YOUR UNIQUE SHAPE AND FORM

Finding tricks to create a flattering body shape is the key to style.
—Stacy London, Cohost, What Not to Wear *on TLC*

Sometimes, when I walk around a crowded place, I find myself carrying an imaginary magic wand and, in my mind, making simple changes to how people are dressed. I wish I had this superpower and could show them, with the tap of a wand, another version of themselves. How amazing they could look with simple tweaks: a tuck here, a bit of length there, maybe a belted waistline, or a different style of pant or jacket.

You will soon have the power to make these adjustments for yourself, trying on new looks for your own reaction and the feedback of others.

If you think of yourself as raw material—a chunk of clay, for example—you can significantly alter the appearance of the shape and size of that clay, your naked being, with the clothes you wear. If you love your bare chunk of clay as is, that is rare and terrific. You will simply want to preserve your shape, being careful not to negatively alter it as you dress. On the other hand, after working with many clients and my own life experience, I am confident that, unfortunately, most of us have a thing or two we'd like to adjust. People commonly want to look leaner, taller, more or less curvy. They have body parts they want to illuminate and areas they wish to de-emphasize.

THE SELF-ASSESSMENT

What about you? Let's start with a self-assessment. What do you love about how you look? Write it down. Is it your eyes, lips, skin, or hair? Don't be shy; you don't have to share it with anyone else. Now, focus on your body. Go to a full-length mirror and look at your naked being from top to bottom, front and back. Do this with a hand mirror so you can fully see the back side of your body. Do it with love and acceptance please. Write down what you like about how you look. I've heard things like shoulders, height, bum, legs, breasts or chest, arms, or legs; you get the point.

Next, and only after you have written a complete list of things you like about your body, if there are things you don't currently appreciate about how you look, write those down too. If you wish your tummy were flatter, you had more curves, or you were thinner and taller and if you don't like your thighs or arms, it's okay to acknowledge it.

This is not a book on how to bulk up, lose weight, or learn about cosmetic treatments to change your body. In this section of the book, however, you will learn how to change how you look in your clothes. But first you need to understand what you want to showcase and what you wish to diminish.

The most significant art element you possess is your body shape. You have probably heard women's bodies referred to as pears, apples, or even bananas. Honestly, I'm not too fond of this. Who feels beautiful thinking of yourself as a piece of fruit? No one! Men have avoided this analogy. Their bodies are compared to actual shapes in art, and that is how it should be done!

Knowing your shape is extremely helpful for dressing your body. It's a tool to help you understand and objectively visualize what clothing shapes will flatter you. It's all about geometry, finding symmetry and balance to be your most aesthetically pleasing. You can celebrate your natural frame or create the illusion of an alternative silhouette simply by adjusting your clothes.

Embracing Your Unique Shape and Form

BODY SHAPES

Men and women have four shapes in common: rectangle, oval, triangle, and inverted triangle (Figure 6.0). Men also have a fifth shape: the trapezoid. Women have a fifth shape: the hourglass.

Figure 6.0

What's the best shape? There is no one answer to this question. Societal standards of beauty vary widely and can change over time. What one finds attractive differs from person to person and culture to culture.

In 2015, Superdrug, a health and beauty retailer in the United Kingdom, wanted to learn more about this. Their project, Perceptions of Perfection Across Borders, was designed to better understand potentially unrealistic beauty standards and see how such pressures vary worldwide. They asked graphic designers from eighteen countries to alter a digital image to depict "ideal beauty" from their culture.[2] The results were fascinating. The designers' edited female body shapes included skinny rectangles, triangles, and, most commonly, thin to voluptuous hourglasses (Figure 6.1).

Superdrug later assigned weight and BMI (body mass index) to the drawn images. The weight of the 5-foot, 5-inch subjects ranged from a skinny 102 pounds with a BMI of 17 in China to a fuller-figured 153 pounds and 25.5 BMI in Spain. The United States, the United Kingdom, Netherlands, Argentina, Philippines, and Mexico landed midpoint at around 128 pounds and a BMI of approximately 21—still an unrealistic size for most women.

The results of that project were so compelling that Superdrug followed up with a similar project for men: Perceptions of Perfection, Part II: Men. It turns out the quest for a perfect body transcends gender. Men feel pressure to be strong, slim, and muscular. As with the women, Superdrug provided sixteen graphic artists worldwide with an image of a man not expected to be the ideal. They gave little instruction and asked the designers to edit the image to illustrate their culture's ideal man's physical traits (Figure 6.2).

In Australia, he maintained his shape for the most part; in the United Kingdom, he got thinner, and of course, the United States was demanding, giving him a very muscular, chiseled appearance. His chest was even more built in Russia and Egypt, making him a true inverted triangle. Similar to women, China's guy was the thinnest. An interesting aside is how much the graphic artists changed not only their ideal man's physique

Perceptions of Perfection - Women

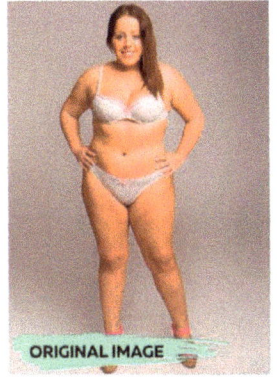

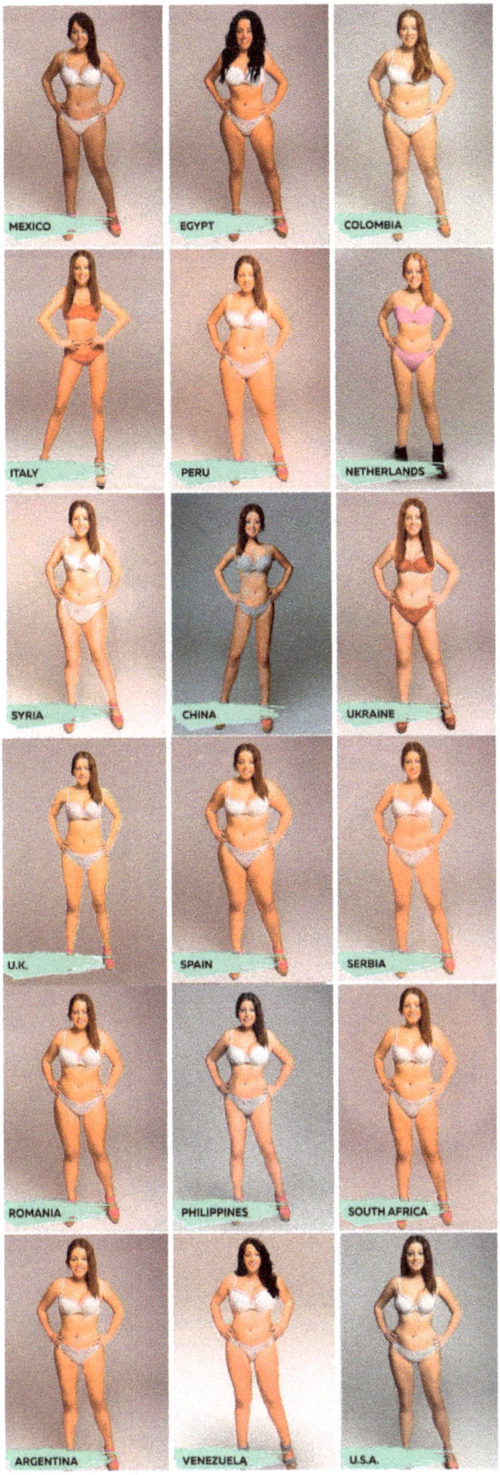

Figure 6.1

YOUR ULTIMATE STYLE BLUEPRINT

Perceptions of Perfection - Men

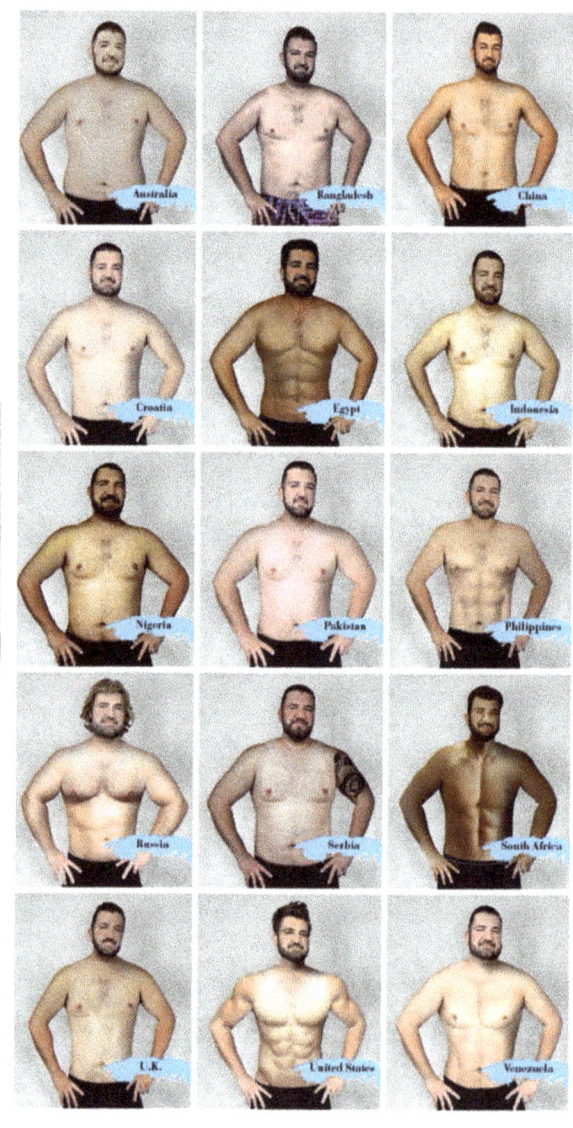

Figure 6.2

Embracing Your Unique Shape and Form

but also his hair and skin tone. Serbia's man even got a tattoo.[3]

What's the best shape to have? As you can see, that's a personal choice. It is crucial to balance your genetics, lifestyle, and preferences. I admit it is hard for me as well, but honoring the body you have is a worthy goal.

You might be happy to learn you aren't alone if you don't possess your ideal body shape. Research shows only 8% of all women have an hourglass shape. Fewer men have their favorite shape: 5% of men are inverted triangles or trapezoids. A rectangle is the most common body shape: 46% of women and 42% of men have this shape. As to the rest, 20% of women and 14% of men are triangles, and just under 14% of women and 26% of men are ovals, leaving approximately 12% of women inverted triangles.[4]

Which shape are you?

- **You are a rectangle** if your shoulders, chest, waist, and hips are basically the same dimensions. Take a look in the mirror or pull out a measuring tape, and if your shoulders, waist, and hips are very close to the same width, you are a rectangle. You could be short and wide, tall and thin, or somewhere in between.
- **You are a triangle** if you are a woman with a very narrow waist, trim upper body, and noticeably wider hips than shoulders. Men have this shape too, although it is less common. If you are a man with this shape, you likely have sloping shoulders and a thin upper body; when you gain weight, it is in your lower abdomen and hips.
- **You are an inverted triangle** if you flip the triangle upside down: your shoulders are broad, and your hips are narrow. Some men work hard in the gym for this shape and build a firm, broad chest and shoulders with a torso that tapers to a thin waist.
- **You are a trapezoid** if you are a man and your waist is narrow, and your chest and shoulders are broad. This gives your body an overall appearance of an inverted trapezoidal shape—a

modified or more subtle inverted triangle.
- **You are an hourglass** if you are a woman with a very small waist, while your shoulders and hips are broader (usually by at least two inches) and even.
- **You are an oval** if you carry your weight in your tummy with trimmer shoulders and legs.

A quick note about body shapes: so far, we have reviewed a flattened version of a human being, which is technically what a shape is. But you are not a cardboard cutout. You are a three-dimensional being. In art, a three-dimensional shape is referred to as a form. Technically, a human body is a form and you could be one shape from the front, another from the back, and a third from the side. For example, it is common for a woman to be an hourglass from the front, but a belly is apparent when she turns sideways, making her an oval from that vantage point. One could also have a full bottom from the back, making them a triangular shape from that viewpoint. For this reason, I recommend you always look at yourself from the side and back as well as from the front.

I find it fascinating that many clients don't own a full-length mirror when we start working together. It's essential to see how you look from head to toe. If you don't own a full-length mirror, pause, go online, and buy one now. Or add it to your shopping list if you prefer to shop in person. While you're at it, ensure you have a hand mirror too. This way, you can easily see your back. Other people see the side and back of you as much as the front. Why not note what they see and ensure you are happy with your full-body presentation?

What should you do with this information? First, decide if you love your shape. Congratulations if you are among the lucky few who embrace their body shape; as I have said before, it is a worthy goal! Regardless, we can all look amazing and create an alternative silhouette by learning how to dress our bodies.

Ironically, most people gravitate to clothes that emphasize their

Embracing Your Unique Shape and Form

natural shape, not the one they desire. Rectangles are commonly drawn to long, boxy styles. Triangles wear tight clothes on top, where they are small, and colorful full pants and skirts on the bottom, where they are fuller. An inverted triangle typically does the opposite, wearing dark, sleek clothes on the bottom, where they are small, and brighter attention-grabbing garments where they are more significant. For men, this can work well. This approach will emphasize their muscular upper body and exaggerate their desired V-shape. However, women don't usually want this silhouette because it is very masculine. Likewise, ovals often dress similarly, with bright, oversized tunics on top and tighter, darker bottoms. When asked why this choice was made, they say they are hiding. But in actuality, they are making what is already large appear larger while removing focus from their legs, which are typically assets.

Ladies, look at Figure 6.3 for examples of what I am talking about and Figure 6.4 for simple shifts that would make all the difference.

Rectangle   Inverted Triangle   Triangle   Oval

YOUR ULTIMATE STYLE BLUEPRINT

Rectangle   Inverted Triangle   Triangle   Oval

Figure 6.3
Figure 6.4

I see common mistakes in men too. Men often wear clothing that is too tight or too baggy, too long or too short in all the wrong places—patterns, stripes, and bold colors directing attention to sensitive areas of their body and tucking in when they have a belly they would like to conceal.

It's intuitive but often overlooked: intentionally draw attention to your best features and away from your least flattering ones. If you have an area to showcase or want to add volume where you are smaller than you wish, the trick is to add interest to that area. Try things like:

- Bright colors
- Horizontal stripes
- Contrasting colors and designs
- Ruffles

- Embellishments
- Bold geometric shapes and patterns
- Statement accessories: jewelry, ties, scarves, pocket squares

If you have an area you want to minimize, do the opposite. Wear comparatively dark, solid basics in these areas.

Following is a list of the common questions my clients ask me related to dressing their body shapes.

FOR THE LADIES

"How can I showcase my waist?"

This question is common for women with hourglass figures. Women with triangle shapes also have tiny waists they want to emphasize. Women who are rectangles or inverted triangles can often create the illusion of a waist. On the other hand, the oval-shaped woman will have the most difficulty with this; she will likely want to bypass her waist. If you are thin overall, you can bring attention to your waist by choosing the following:

- Dresses that are belted, have waistlines, or cinch at the waist
- Bolero jackets, peplum jackets, or others that taper at the waist
- Blouses with waistbands, belts or ties, peplum tops, wrap tops, and others that taper at the waist
- Flair pants

Tucking fitted blouses and shirts into high-waisted pants and skirts is also flattering. Check out Figure 6.5 for examples.

YOUR ULTIMATE STYLE BLUEPRINT

Figure 6.5

If you have a waist but also a tummy to conceal:

- Search for dresses, jackets, and tops with ruching that will bring attention to your waist without directly accentuating it.
- Wear bolero sweaters and jackets that will bring attention to your waist without spotlighting it.
- Avoid baggy clothing or anything that bypasses your waist. This will add bulk to your overall appearance, which is the opposite of your goal.

"Can I make my tummy disappear?"

This is a common question. Especially as we age, all body types can develop a tummy we never had before. Consider these tactics to remove attention from your midsection:

- Wear darker, solid-colored tops and jackets.
- Drop-waisted dresses and tops that aren't too snug can be a good option.
- Empire-waisted tops and dresses can be flattering, but be careful; some can accentuate the tummy, making you appear pregnant.
- Choose wide-legged pants, which can surprisingly offset weight gain in your stomach area and make you look more balanced. Many women, especially ovals, combine leggings or skinny pants with oversized tunics, thinking they are hiding their midsection and showcasing their legs. This doesn't work. It makes what is small smaller and what is big bigger. I call this the popsicle effect. Instead, reverse this with snug but not too tight dark-colored tops and wider-legged fuller bottoms. Refer back to Figures 6.3 and 6.4.
- Find shirts and jackets that fit you just right, not too snug

around the middle, and are long enough to cover your stomach. Raise your hands above your head to ensure it's the right fit. You likely don't want us to see your naked tummy if you are working to conceal it.
- Also, shirts that don't have a blunt line on the bottom but are concave or convex in design will elongate your body and help you look thinner.
- Wear straight skirts, not pencil skirts, which may be too snug around your middle.
- Tops with embellishments will bring attention to your face.
- Avoid bright and high-contrasting colors around your middle.
- Avoid long necklaces that land at the tummy—it's like putting a bullseye right where you don't want people to look.
- Wear off-the-shoulder tops, dresses, and cold-shoulder blouses with a cutout in the arms.
- Short skirts and dresses that show off your legs are a great choice.

For some specific items to add to your closet, check out Figure 6.6.

"How do I look curvier?"

This question comes up most often with women who have a rectangular shape, and it's worth noting that this is the most common female figure. Creating curves is as much about what not to do as what to do:

- Wear jeans and slacks with a gentle flare or bootcut; avoid severe tapered pants, leggings, and skinny jeans because they will tend to enhance your straight lines.
- Look for tops and jackets with round, scoop necks and a convex bottom rather than a straight cut and anything cropped or boxy.
- Consider the half-tucked blouse to create a concave bottom.

Embracing Your Unique Shape and Form

Figure 6.6

- Stick to rounded patterns and circular jewelry; avoid straight lines, square designs, and patterns; they will bring attention to your natural straight lines. This will be covered in depth in Chapter 12, "Complete Your Look: The Art of Accessorizing."
- See Figure 6.7 for some specifics. Also refer back to Figure 6.5; things that emphasize the waist typically help a straight, narrow woman look curvier.

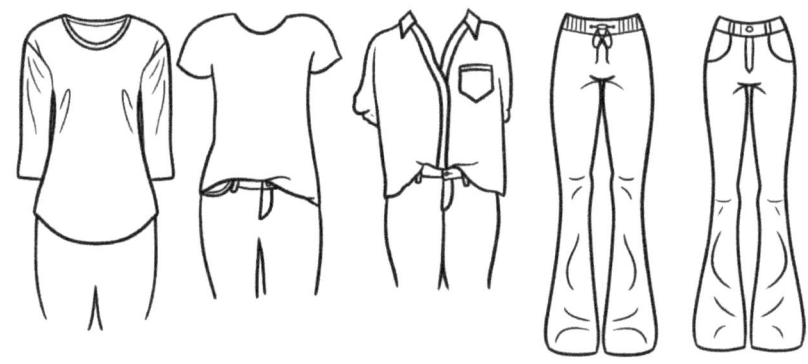

Figure 6.7

"Can you help my hips and thighs appear smaller?"

This question is most common for the triangle body shape. Consider this:

- Tops with ruffles, cap sleeves, patterns, bright colors, embellishments, or off-the-shoulder necklines bring attention away from your hips and thighs and to your slim upper body.
- Tops and jackets that cinch at the waist, are tied or belted, and are not too narrow around the hips will emphasize your thin waist without bringing attention to the hips and thighs.
- Bolero and cropped tops will also bring attention to your waist and away from your hips and thighs.
- Pants and skirts in solid colors with a flat panel—no pleats,

Embracing Your Unique Shape and Form

ruffles, or side pockets—will minimize your bottom half.
- Wide-legged pants, palazzo pants, and pants with a flare cut will balance out wider hips and thighs.
- A-line skirts and fit-and-flare dresses showcase your waist while concealing your hips and thighs.
- Remember to avoid anything that bypasses your trim upper body and waist, such as tunic tops and shift dresses.
- Avoid anything with bright colors, contrasting patterns, or ruffles below your waist; it will bring unwanted attention to that area.

For some specific examples, take a look at Figure 6.8. As a side note, if you love skinny straight pants or already own some and want to keep them in your closet, I recommend shoes or boots with color or bulk. This will add visual weight and, by comparison, diminish your hips. Also, if you are a triangle, finding pants that fit off the rack may be challenging due to your thin waist. Buy pants that fit your hips and thighs perfectly, and hire a sewist who can take them in to fit your waistline.

YOUR ULTIMATE STYLE BLUEPRINT

Figure 6.8

Embracing Your Unique Shape and Form

"I'm top-heavy; what do I do?"

This question is typically asked by females with an inverted triangle shape. Fortunately, this is easy to remedy by adding visual weight to your bottom, immediately creating a more symmetrical and balanced look. Unlike most other body shapes, you look great in fun, full, bright patterns and fabrics below the waist. Let's start with your list of what not to do. Avoid these:

- Off-the-shoulder necklines or sleeves with cutouts, which will make you look broader
- Tops with ruffles around the shoulders, cap sleeves, and other designs that bring attention to your shoulders
- Tunics and baggy tops, which will make you look larger, especially if you pair them with skinny jeans or extremely tapered pants
- Jackets with shoulder pads

Try these instead:

- Minimize your upper body by wearing dark, solid colors above the waist.
- Wear pants and skirts with visual weight: contrasting patterns and bright colors.
- Consider wider-legged pants to balance out your upper body.
- Wear tops that are loose but not bulky.
- Accessorize with scarves, necklaces, and earrings to draw attention to your face and away from your shoulders and chest.

See Figure 6.9 for examples of wardrobe essentials to minimize a chest and broad shoulders.

YOUR ULTIMATE STYLE BLUEPRINT

Figure 6.9

Embracing Your Unique Shape and Form

FOR THE MEN

With the gents, I get fewer questions about their shape. The two most common are how to diminish a belly and how to look more like a trapezoid or inverted triangle. Let's tackle the second one first.

"How do I dress to create more of a V-shaped body?"

If you want more of a trapezoid or inverted triangle shape, focus on creating interest at your chest and shoulders and tapering at the waist. Try these tips:

- Wear blazers with structured shoulders and consider attention-grabbing patterns and colors that will emphasize your upper body even more.
- Choose single-breasted suits with structured shoulders and cinched-in waists, not double-breasted jackets (unless you are very tall and thin and want to add overall width). See Figure 6.10 for examples of men's jacket types and lapels.

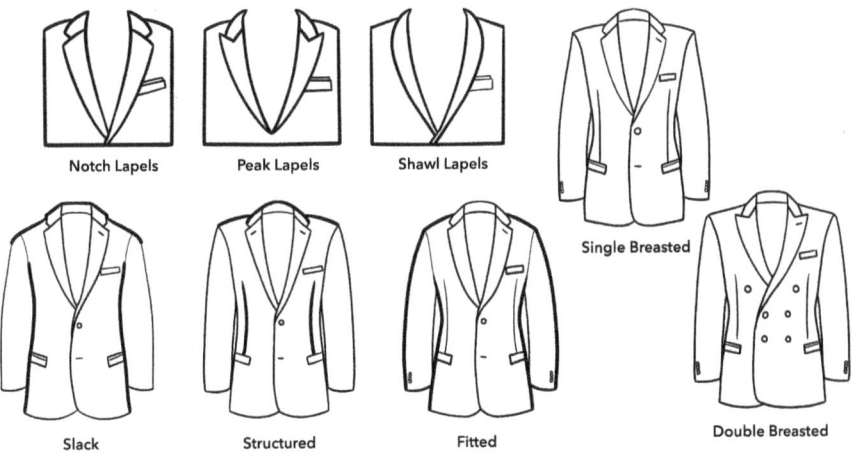

Figure 6.10

YOUR ULTIMATE STYLE BLUEPRINT

- Wear shirts with horizontal stripes, bright or bold colors, or other details across your upper torso to draw attention to that area. Ensure your shirts either taper at the waist or are tucked into your pants.
- Button-down shirts layered under crew neck sweaters work well.
- Consider statement accessories like pocket squares, interesting ties, neck scarves, and necklaces. See Figure 6.11 for examples of tops and jackets that direct the eye to the chest and upper body.

Figure 6.11

Embracing Your Unique Shape and Form

- You may also diminish your lower body with straight-legged, dark, and solid-colored pants.
- Avoid clothes that are too tight, baggy, or boxy, as well as jackets with unstructured shoulders.
- Stay away from bomber jackets or similar with slouchy shoulders.
- Stay away from pants in brighter colors, busy prints, and statement belts, because these will only draw attention to the width of your waist. Also avoid pants with pleats or skinny fits. See Figure 6.12 for examples of men's trouser styles

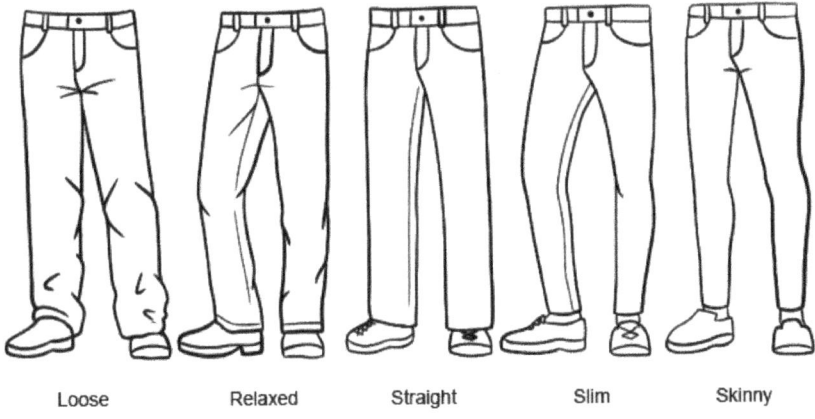

Loose   Relaxed   Straight   Slim   Skinny

Figure 6.12

"I'm too thick in the middle; what can I do?"

- Choose single-breasted jackets in dark colors and only slightly tapered. Double-breasted jackets will add to your weight. Refer back to Figure 6.10 for examples of men's jacket types and lapels.
- Tailor shirts so they fit just right.
- V-neck shirts with long sleeves will create the illusion of a slimmer silhouette, cowl necks can add volume to the upper body, and wide crew-neck shirts are also slenderizing.

- Avoid large prints and contrasting patterns; they attract unwanted attention to a larger midriff. Horizontal stripes should also be avoided.
- Be mindful of tucking in your shirts—untucked shirts that aren't too boxy will be more flattering.
- Layer up. Shirt jackets and blazers over T-shirts minimize your midsection while adding sophistication to your style.
- Consider wearing some accessories. Bow ties will bring attention upward. If you aren't a fan of this look, wear a wide tie long enough to reach your belt. Thin belts are better than wide ones. Also, pocket squares or a statement necklace with more casual looks can help avert the eye from your middle and toward your chest, shoulders, and face.
- Depending on your size, suspenders may be a good choice. They hold the trouser front out slightly, helping the fit appear smoother. They can be hidden under a jacket, vest, or sweater or used as an accessory in a contrasting color. Regardless, they should be worn in a straight line from your shoulders to your waist.
- Consider pants with bright colors and patterns if your legs are thinner than your midsection. This will add visual weight to your legs and balance out your shape.
- Opt for an elongated effect: dress in monochromatic colors from top to bottom.
- Consider flat-panel, wide-legged trousers. Straight-leg jeans or tapered slacks may overemphasize your tummy.
- Also, avoid low-rise jeans or trousers that sit below the belly. They elongate the torso, making the stomach appear larger and the legs look shorter.

If you are a man with the coveted trapezoid shape, dressing and finding clothes should be easier for you. The trapezoid, which is not average at all, is often called the "average shape" because fashion designers commonly use it as their fit model. This means you have the added convenience of many clothes fitting you off the rack. Most styles will look good on you, so your list of what not to wear is short. Most colors and patterns should work well with your build. This allows you to have lots of options. In general, your best wardrobe items are as follows:

- Trousers and pants with a close fit unless you have very thin legs, in which case you will want a wider-leg pant.
- Bootcut jeans
- Blazers and suit jackets that taper at your waist
- Neckties: Stick to a standard length (the tip should be right around your belt buckle) and a standard width (about three to three-and-a-half inches). Short, skinny, fat, or otherwise oddly sized ties throw off the balance of your torso.

Consider avoiding these items:

- Baggy clothes
- Skinny jeans, which will make you proportionately too narrow below the belt

BUCKING THE TRENDS

But what about the trends? What if your ideal pants, jackets, or tops are not in style? This can be an issue. We can't get around the fact that the fashion industry changes what's in fashion every season, influencing inventory. But know this: everything I have recommended, no matter your body shape, is always available; they are classic pieces. They will be more readily available at certain times versus others, but you can find them. You don't need to be held captive by the fashion industry. You can dress your body first and the trends second. With that said, if you want to be trendy, even modern, adding a few new pieces every year that illustrate that you are current and relevant is a good practice.

YOUR ULTIMATE STYLE BLUEPRINT

Remember, regardless of gender, size, or body shape, the goal is to love how you look and dress to communicate your personality and values. If you find a piece of clothing or an outfit that breaks a style rule but leaves you feeling inspired and empowered, wear it! Just be sure that you look at yourself in the mirror from a 360-degree vantage point and that you love what you see.

What is your body shape from the front, side, and back? What did you learn from the questions others have asked about how to dress their body shape? It's time to update Your Ultimate Style Blueprint Summary Sheet. If you haven't already done so, you can download it from my website's Resources page: https://successthrustyle.com/resources/my-style-blueprint.

Chapter 7

BALANCING ACT: STYLING YOUR BODY'S UNIQUE PROPORTIONS

Proportions are what make the old Greek temples classic in their beauty. It is the same with the human body; if the proportions are harmonious, the result is a great beauty.

—Commonly attributed to Leonardo da Vinci

Have you ever wondered if you are short-waisted, long-waisted, short-legged, or long-legged? Are you uncertain which jacket length is best for you? Would you like to appear leaner and taller? Dressing your body proportions can transform your appearance, and it's something most people don't understand. They assume all they need to consider is if they are tall, average, or petite. In fact, it's all relative. Your proportions, the answer to these questions and more, are related to your head size. It's honestly mind-blowing. I have a client who had some pretty unkind words for her face and always complained that it was too long. Her head is nine inches, which is indeed long for a typical woman, but she is also six feet tall. Her body would likely appear lanky, awkward, and out of proportion if her head were shorter. When I pointed this out, she started to see herself in a new light.

Our understanding of body proportions was introduced around 1487 by Leonardo da Vinci and is depicted in his world-famous Vitruvian Man (Figure 7.0).[1]

YOUR ULTIMATE STYLE BLUEPRINT

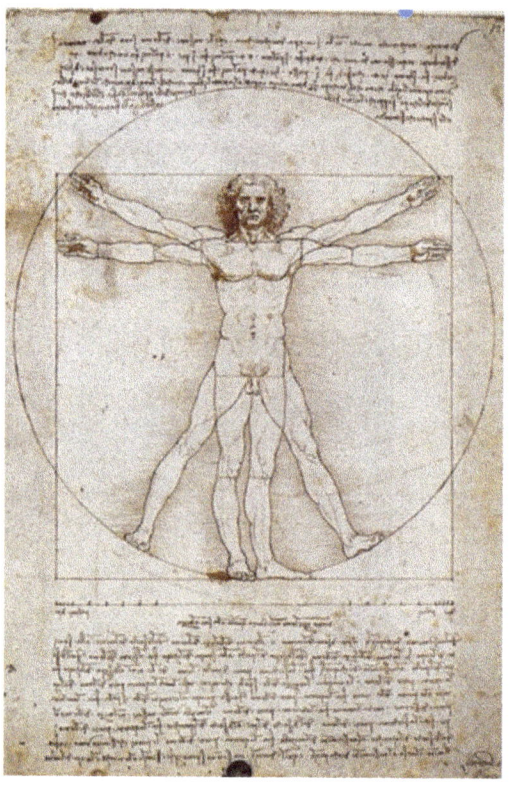

Figure 7.0

Sometimes called the Canon of Proportions or the Proportions of Man, this pen-and-ink drawing, inspired by the famed architect Vitruvius, exemplifies Leonardo's interest in defining perfect human body proportions. The drawing illustrates the relationship of human proportions to mathematics, specifically phi, commonly known as the golden ratio or golden mean. As mentioned in the introduction to this section, math is connected to beauty through this golden ratio, which is considered the standard for universal beauty. It creates a balanced relationship that the mind's eye finds especially aesthetically pleasing. We will use this knowledge in this chapter and relate it to your body. Specifically, we will assess

Balancing Act: Styling Your Body's Unique Proportions

the length of your body relative to your head and individual body parts and how to dress based on this knowledge.

In his notes associated with Vitruvian Man, Leonardo wrote, "From the bottom of the chin to the top of the head is one-eighth of a man's height."[2] In other words, our bodies are proportionate when we are eight head lengths. You may have noticed that artists often start by drawing a stack of eight ovals when they draw the human form (Figure 7.1).

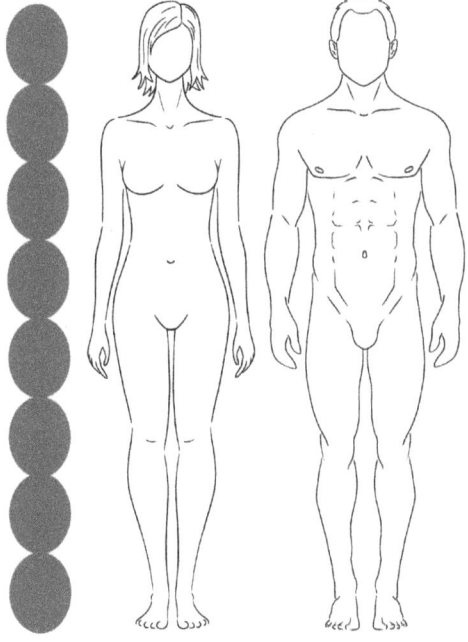

Figure 7.1

The size of each oval is determined by each individual's head size, and our body parts are proportional and proportionally relative to each of us individually. If you have a small head, your waist, hips, and legs can be shorter and still proportionate. If you have a longer head, you will look more balanced if your body parts are longer.

Knowing your proportions will inform what wardrobe items will make you look the most balanced and, thus, attractive. The trick is to compensate with short or long clothing in the same way you learned to adjust for your body shape in the last chapter. It's simple geometry.

My experience working with women and men of all sizes has taught me that very few of us have ideal proportions. If you are fortunate enough to have a body that is eight head lengths (and therefore balanced with your head), it is likely your body parts—waist, hips, rise, and legs—are not proportionate. So learning to create the illusion of this symmetry can bring you back to balance and help you look thinner and taller if that is the goal.

HEAD LENGTH AND PROPORTION

Start by measuring your head (Figure 7.2). This is your most critical measurement since everything else relates to it. The best way to do this is to stand with even weight on both feet. Hold a measuring tape straight up and down from the crown of your head to the bottom of your chin. I recommend having someone do this for you; if not, use a mirror as your aide to ensure your measuring tape is straight.

A typical head length ranges between 7 and 9.5 inches. Once you have that number, you can determine if your head is proportionate with your body by manually measuring your body. You can do this by taking the measuring tape down your body in increments of your head length. For example, if your head is 8 inches, you will measure the rest of your body seven times, in 8-inch intervals, starting at the bottom of your chin. Alternatively, if you are sure of your height, you can divide your head length by your height. Following our example, if your head is 8 inches and you are 5 feet, 5 inches (65 inches), you would learn that you are 8.125 head lengths—pretty darn close to being proportionate. If, on the other hand, you are 5 feet, 3 inches, your body is short for your head, and if you are 6 feet, your body is long for your head. See Figure 7.3 to label your head and body measurements.

Balancing Act: Styling Your Body's Unique Proportions

Figure 7.2

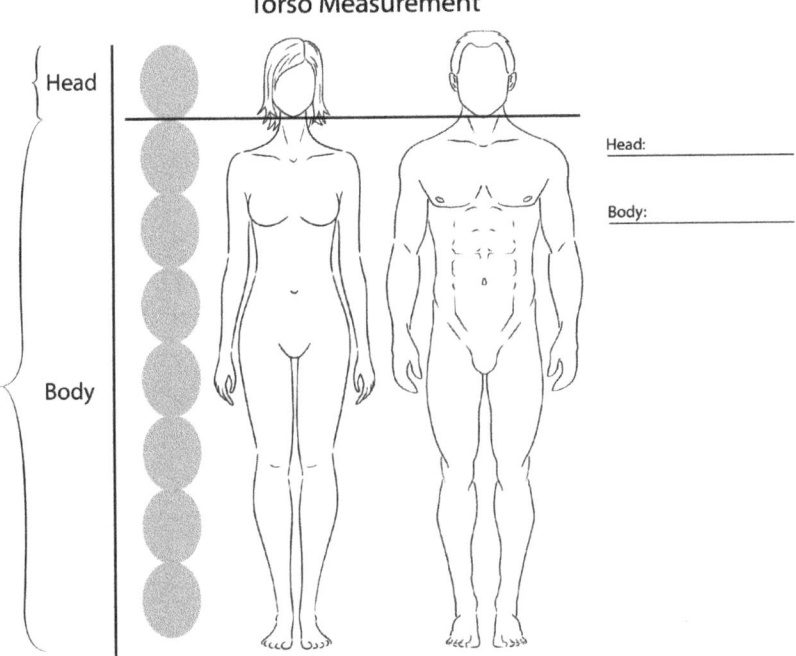

Figure 7.3

ADJUSTING FOR OVERALL BODY PROPORTIONS

If you learned your body is short for your head, you can elongate your overall appearance. Take a look at Figure 7.4. One fantastic trick, an optical illusion, is to shorten your sleeve length. Simply stated, when we show more arm, we look taller.

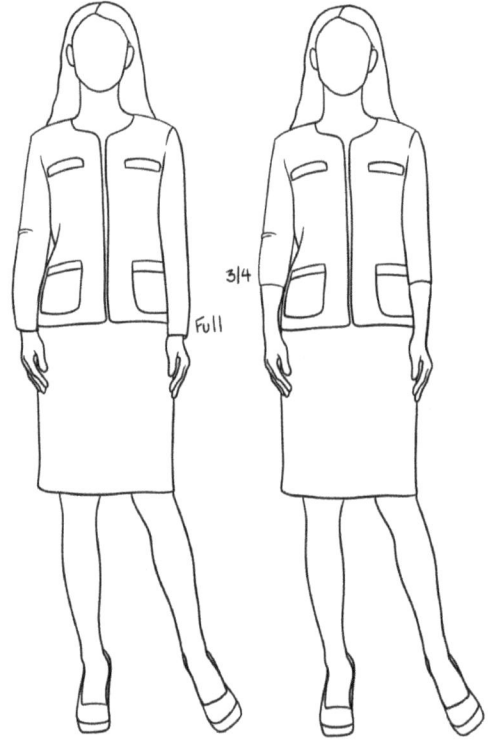

Figure 7.4

Ladies, blouses, dresses, and jackets with three-quarter-length sleeves are readily available. If you own something or find the perfect item with long sleeves, it can easily be altered. On the other hand, the three-quarter-length sleeve is rare for men. But don't despair; both men and women can roll up long-sleeved shirts, often called shushing, to create the three-quarter-length look. However, if your body is long for your head, this look will make you look even longer and potentially awkward and lanky. Given the option, you may prefer long sleeves to three-quarter sleeves.

Something else to consider is the shoulder width of your jackets. Jacket shoulders frame your head. If the jacket's shoulders are narrow, your head will appear disproportionately large. The opposite is true for jacket's with wide shoulders. Look at Figure 7.5. Can you see how the man's head in the wide jacket appears smaller than the man's head in the narrow jacket? Play around with this and see what works for your body and which shoulder widths are most flattering.

Wide   Narrow

Figure 7.5

Monochromatic dressing—wearing the same color from head to toe or simply sticking to all dark-toned clothing—is another way to elongate your appearance. This is also extremely slimming, as seen in Figure 7.6.

YOUR ULTIMATE STYLE BLUEPRINT

Figure 7.6

A variation of this concept is column dressing, which involves wearing monochromatic colors except for a jacket or sweater in another color, as shown in Figure 7.7.

Balancing Act: Styling Your Body's Unique Proportions

Figure 7.7

Conversely, the more you break up your silhouette with color and contrast, the more the effect is reduced. Compare Figure 7.8 to Figures 7.6 and 7.7.

YOUR ULTIMATE STYLE BLUEPRINT

Figure 7.8

Another approach to bringing your proportionally short body in balance would be to make your head appear shorter. This is less commonly desirable. However, if this is your goal it can be achieved through your hairstyle. We will cover hairstyles in more detail in Chapter 11, but as your hair

Balancing Act: Styling Your Body's Unique Proportions

relates to your proportions, consider how much height and visual weight (length and color) your hairstyle adds to or reduces your overall appearance. The more height and visual weight, the larger your head will appear, and the less color contrast and volume in your hair, the smaller it will appear. Finally, wearing tall hats is another excellent way to elongate your head (more on hats in Chapter 12).

If you learned your body is long for your head, refer back to Figure 7.8 to discover how to shorten the appearance of your body. However, remember this approach may also add width to your frame, making you appear heavier than you are. Wearing cropped pants (or at least pants with a shorter break), flats, and separates of varying colors are the best ways to shorten a proportionately long body. If you are concerned with your size and feeling thinner, that may be more important than looking proportionate. In this case, I suggest you reread the previous paragraph and simply consider hairstyles to add height to your head, and embrace your long body.

ADJUSTING FOR WAIST PROPORTIONS

Even if you are one of the lucky few whose head and body are perfectly proportionate, you might find that your body parts—your waist, rise (the space between your groin and waistline), and legs—are not.

Let's return to our example of the eight head lengths and the drawing of eight stacked ovals to determine if your waist is balanced with the rest of your body. Your waistline should ideally measure at the bottom of the third head length or oval. In our example, that would be sixteen inches below the chin. When you measure, if you aren't sure you landed at your waistline, do a side bend and see where that is on your body. If your waist is above that measurement, you are short-waisted. If your waist is below that measurement, you are long-waisted.

Take a look at Figure 7.9 to help assess and record your waist measurement.

YOUR ULTIMATE STYLE BLUEPRINT

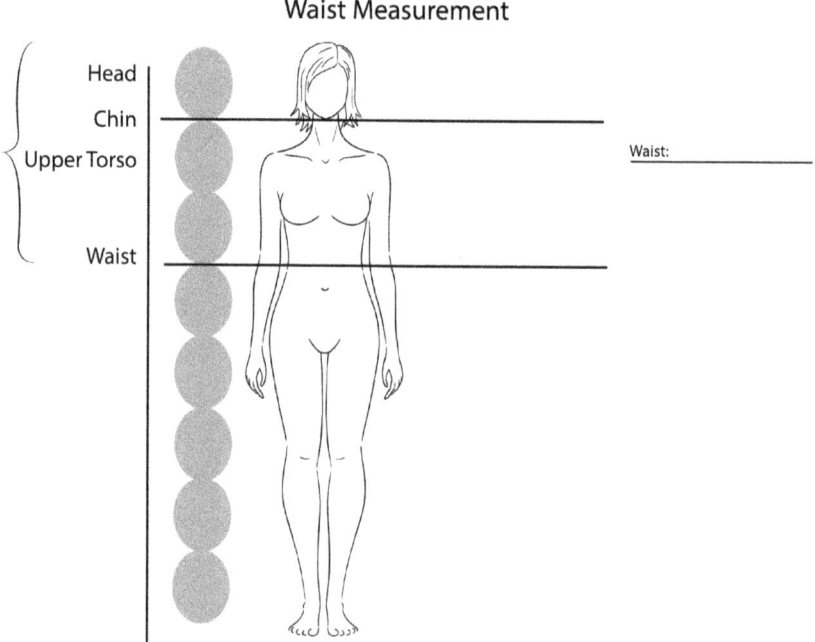

Figure 7.9

As we move forward, it is important to note that you only need to worry about using clothes to create the illusion of a shorter or longer waist if it is visibly noticeable and bothers you. If you measure an inch longer or shorter than your ideal proportions would indicate but have never noticed this issue and are not concerned about it, jump to the next section. For this example and the others, only focus on tips to fix things that trouble you or impact your self-confidence.

Balancing Act: Styling Your Body's Unique Proportions

Are you are a short-waisted woman?

In this case you likely want to make your waist appear longer. You should know this:

- Drop-waisted tops and dresses will lower your perceived waistline.
- Empire waist and flowy dresses and tops with no waistline will similarly conceal your high waistline.
- Belts below your waist will also lower your waistline.
- Longer jackets can extend the appearance of your upper body.
- Mid-rise pants will be your most flattering and comfortable choice; high-rise slacks and jeans will emphasize your short waist and likely be uncomfortable.
- Dresses that aren't belted or have a definite waistline will make your short waist unnoticeable, so they're a great choice.
- Rompers and jumpsuits can do the same; however, you may need to alter the inseam to fit you properly.
- Monochromatic colors or at least similar tones will help elongate your waist compared to high-contrast separates, which bring attention to your short waist.
- Tops and jackets with convex bottoms will help lengthen your torso, which is additionally very slenderizing.

Coincidentally, the same tactics used to minimize a tummy also bypass the waistline, thus concealing it. So refer back to Figure 6.6 because all those options apply. You can also refer to Figure 7.6 for tips on monochromatic dressing. Finally, look at Figure 7.10 for examples of how using blazers can focus on your short waist or lengthen it.

YOUR ULTIMATE STYLE BLUEPRINT

Figure 7.10

 A common question for short-waisted ladies is how to showcase a waist and lengthen it simultaneously. As you can see in many examples of ways to lengthen your waistline, it is bypassed altogether. This is because it can be a challenge to both show your waist and lengthen it. If you have a tummy to conceal, this will work out perfectly. But if you have a waist and look best in clothes that show your shape, you may decide that is more important than elongating your short waist. You can certainly do both, but the options are more limited. Your best bet is to look for tops and dresses that cinch in at the sides and avoid boxy cuts. Take a look at Figure 7.11 for a few ideas.

Balancing Act: Styling Your Body's Unique Proportions

Figure 7.11

Are you are a long-waisted woman?

Consider this:

- Wide belts can shorten your waistline.
- Dresses are a great choice as they commonly avoid your waistline. However, be mindful that a dress with a belt or waistline may not fit you correctly.
- Short or crop-length jackets and tops will visually raise your waistline.
- High-waisted pants or skirts will extend your leg length and make your waist appear shorter and more balanced.
- Paper bag-style pants create the appearance of a high waist.
- One-piece outfits like jumpsuits and rompers may also avoid your waist. However, many have built-in waistlines, and the

inseam may need to be longer and, therefore, will need to be altered to fit you correctly.
- Monochromatic colors or at least similar tones will help draw attention away from your waist, compared to high-contrast separates, which will bring attention to your long waist.
- Your naturally lower waistline can create the appearance of shorter legs; you can offset this by wearing vertical stripes below the waist, and heels.
- Tucking in your tops will help create a higher waist and make your legs appear longer. Additionally, many long-waisted women struggle to find tops of suitable length; tucking in is a way to make it work, even if a shirt is shorter than ideal.

Figure 7.12 will help you visualize some of these concepts.

Figure 7.12

Balancing Act: Styling Your Body's Unique Proportions

PROPORTIONS IN MEN

For men, we think more in terms of torso and legs. We clearly aren't focused on showing the waist to create that hourglass figure. Instead, we think of men's proportions in terms of their torso and inseam. The first four head lengths are from the top of the head to the groin, and the next four are from the groin to the floor. See Figure 7.13 to gather your measurements.

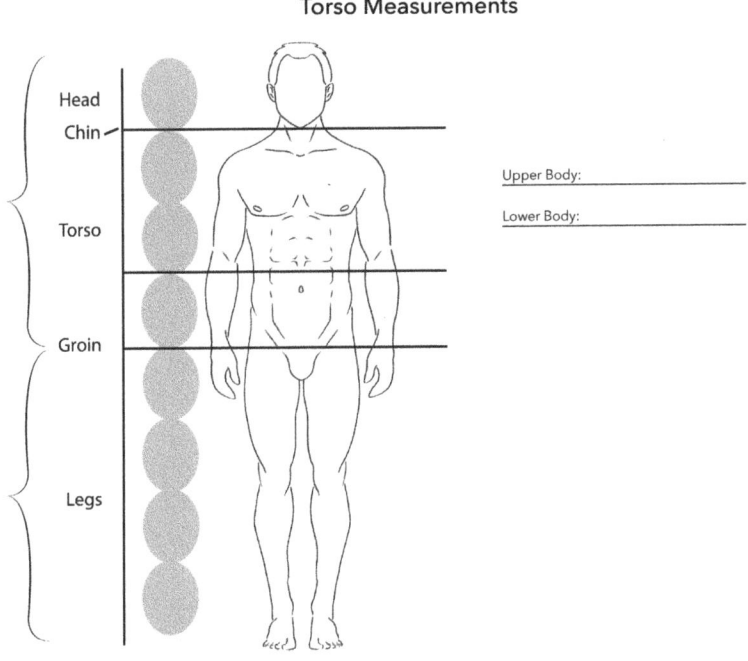

Figure 7.13

The most prominent way men impact the appearance of their torso is through the choice of indoor jacket: sport coat, blazer, or suit jacket. These essential wardrobe items should be carefully considered in terms of length, width, lapels, buttons, and fit. Additional aspects like color, fabric, and texture are also important and will be explored in future chapters.

The difference between a sport coat, blazer, and suit jacket lies in their level of formality, fabric, styling details, and intended use.

- Sport Coat: The most casual of the three, a sport coat is typically made from textured, durable fabrics such as tweed, herringbone, or flannel and often features patterns like plaids or checks, though it may also be solid. Designed to pair with trousers of different materials or colors, sport coats frequently include casual details such as patch pockets or elbow patches.
- Blazer: More formal than a sport coat yet still versatile, a blazer is often a solid color (traditionally navy) and is distinguished by contrasting buttons, often metal. Blazers are typically crafted from smooth fabrics, providing a polished look that pairs well with a variety of outfits, from business-casual to smart-casual.
- Suit Jacket: The most formal of the three, a suit jacket is designed to match a pair of trousers made from the same fabric and color, forming a complete suit. These jackets are typically made from finer, smooth fabrics, and while they may come in a range of colors and patterns, they are most commonly associated with professional and formal settings.

Take a look at Figure 7.14. to see the various types of men's jackets.

Balancing Act: Styling Your Body's Unique Proportions

Figure 7.14

Ideally a man's jacket divides the distance from the collar to the floor roughly in half, creating a balanced, proportionate look. This is called the "half-break" and it's a classic guideline used to achieve visual harmony in a jacket's length. See Figure 7.15. Of course, this rule is adaptable based on personal style and body proportions as most men are not naturally proportionate. The goal is to maintain balance and elongate the figure, so while the half-way rule is a great starting point, slight adjustments can be made based on the man's height, proportions, and style preferences.

Figure 7.15

YOUR ULTIMATE STYLE BLUEPRINT

Are you are a man with a short torso?

Consider the following tips regarding your suit jackets and blazers:

- The best-fitting jacket is long enough to cover the curvature of your buttocks while giving your legs as long a line as possible. A longer jacket will elongate your torso but may shorten your legs.
- The waist button is a delicate balancing act; if you raise it too high, your torso will appear short; if you lower it too much, your torso will appear long. Therefore, a good balance is usually found when the waist button is slightly above your navel.
- Avoid high-buttoning jackets; go with a two-button, single-breasted jacket, drawing the eye downward and making the torso look longer.
- Another jacket consideration is to raise the lapel notches a bit higher. This is typically a more formal look; it will create the illusion of a longer body for the appropriate occasion.

Look at Figure 7.16 to see the best way to wear suit jackets that will elongate your torso, and refer back to Figure 7.14 for an illustration of the most common lapels.

Other considerations for a man with a short torso:

- Wear vertical stripes above the waist, whether in a pinstripe suit or bold stripes in casual wear.
- Choose jeans and slacks with a lower rise.
- Try untucking your shirts, but be sure not to make them too long unless your legs are too long for your body. For this reason, shirts designed to be untucked are your best bet.
- Wear a lighter or brighter shirt with darker-colored pants. This will bring attention to your upper body and diminish your legs.
- When you do tuck in, make sure your belt matches the color of your pants.

Balancing Act: Styling Your Body's Unique Proportions

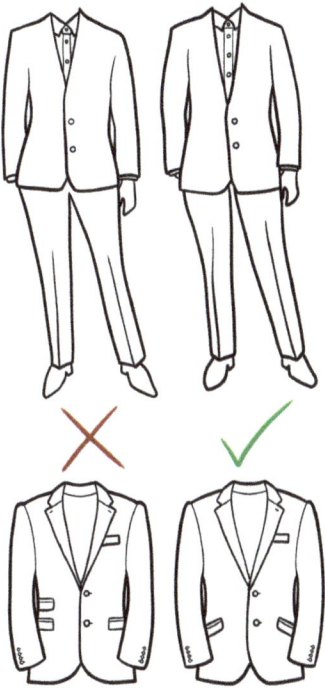

Figure 7.16

Are you a man with a long torso?

Your tips for jackets and blazers are as follows:
- As I mentioned above, the best-fitting jacket is long enough to cover the curvature of your buttocks while giving your legs as long a line as possible. One of the easiest ways to rebalance top-to-bottom proportions for a long torso is to cut the jacket slightly higher than usual—the reverse of what is recommended for the gent with a short torso.
- The waist button is best at your natural navel.
- Where I suggested a longer shirt opening and lower buttons for the man with a short torso, now we want the opposite.

- Low lapels will create more balance for you.
- A patterned jacket to break up the length of your upper body can also work well.

Look at Figure 7.17 for the best way to wear suit jackets to offset your long body.

Other considerations for a man with a long torso:

- Wear shirts and sweaters with a pattern.
- Tuck in your shirts.
- Consider higher-waisted slacks and jeans.
- For casual looks, consider a shorter jacket; bomber jackets are ideal.

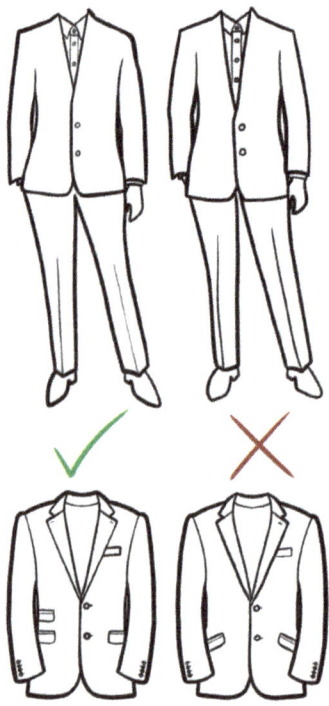

Figure 7.17

Balancing Act: Styling Your Body's Unique Proportions

MEASURING AND ADJUSTING FOR RISE

Your rise is the area between your waist and your groin. It is perfectly proportionate with your head if it is one head length. For example, if your head is eight inches, a proportionate rise would also be eight inches. Measuring this is tricky. You can measure from your waist to your groin if your waist is proportionate. But if it isn't, you want to measure from "where your waist should be." One way to do this is to count down four head lengths from the crown of your head or three head lengths from the bottom of your chin. If your groin is at least very close to this point, your rise is proportionate, and you can move on to the next section. If, on the other hand, the measurement comes up short, your rise is proportionately long for your body, and if the measurement is long, your rise is short. See Figure 7.18 to record the length of your rise.

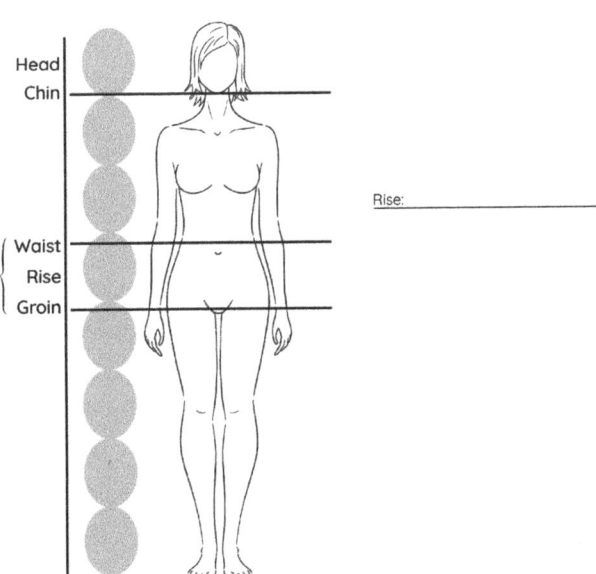

Figure 7.18

Remember that your waist measurement, long or short, can impact the appearance of your rise. For example, if you are short-waisted, you may appear to have a long rise because the distance from your waist to your groin is long. If you are both high-waisted and have a long rise, the effects will be even more exaggerated. Similarly, if you are both long-waisted and have a short rise, your rise may appear even shorter. You will notice that many of the suggestions for someone who is short-waisted and someone with a long rise are similar. The same is true for the long-waisted individual with a short rise.

Did your measurements indicate that your rise is short?

In this case, you can try these techniques to lengthen it visually:

- Wear high-waisted pants and skirts.
- Consider the paper bag pant style.
- Combine these with your tops tucked in.
- Choose shorter tops and jackets.
- Dress in monochromatic colors.
- Wear jackets and tops with a convex bottom.

You saw examples of all of these suggestions earlier in the chapter.

Do you have a long rise?

This is much more common than a proportional or short rise. Therefore, I have many ideas to help you reduce the length of your rise. Consider these options:

- Many dresses bypass your rise.
- Similar to dresses, skirts may be easier to wear than pants; they will be more comfortable and conceal a long rise.
- Pockets, patterns, and details around your hips will optically shorten this area.
- Layered looks help break up the space in a long rise.
- Empire waists are an excellent choice because they bypass your rise.

Balancing Act: Styling Your Body's Unique Proportions

Look at Figure 7.19 for all the ways you can wear jackets, dresses, and tops to break up the space around your rise to help it appear shorter.

Figure 7.19

In addition, belts are valuable tools for creating the illusion of a shortened rise (Figure 7.20).

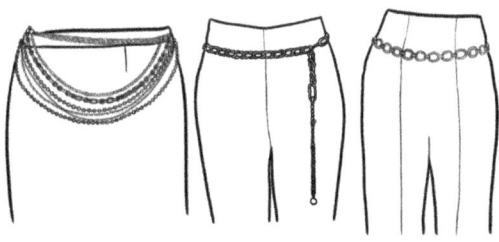

Figure 7.20

Tops that land at your hip bone—the midpoint between your waist and rise—are ideal compared to long tunics or sweaters. Similarly, avoid tucking in your tops, which will emphasize a long rise. Look at Figure 7.21 to see the right length of tops for a long rise.

Keep in mind that fashion trends don't follow these rules. As I write this, in the spring of 2024, the high-waisted pant with a cropped or tucked-in top is all the rage. But as you can see in Figure 7.21, it's not proportionate. For almost all women, this look makes their torso appear incredibly long. It can also make the breasts and buttocks look large. That may be the point. I encourage you to decide for yourself; follow your style guidelines, not the trends. But that doesn't mean you can't break the rules and make your own fashion statement from time to time.

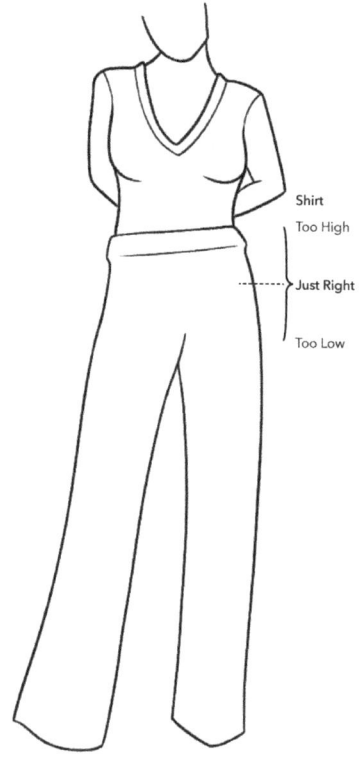

Figure 7.21

LEG PROPORTIONS

The length of your legs, also called your inseam, is proportionate when your legs are four head lengths, which is measured from your groin to the floor. If you want to be precise, well-balanced adult legs are two head lengths to the bottom of your knees and another two head lengths to the floor. Again, measuring this by yourself can be awkward, so find a companion to help or try sitting down. Another option would be to take these instructions to a sewist and ask them to take all your measurements. See Figure 7.22 to record the length of your legs.

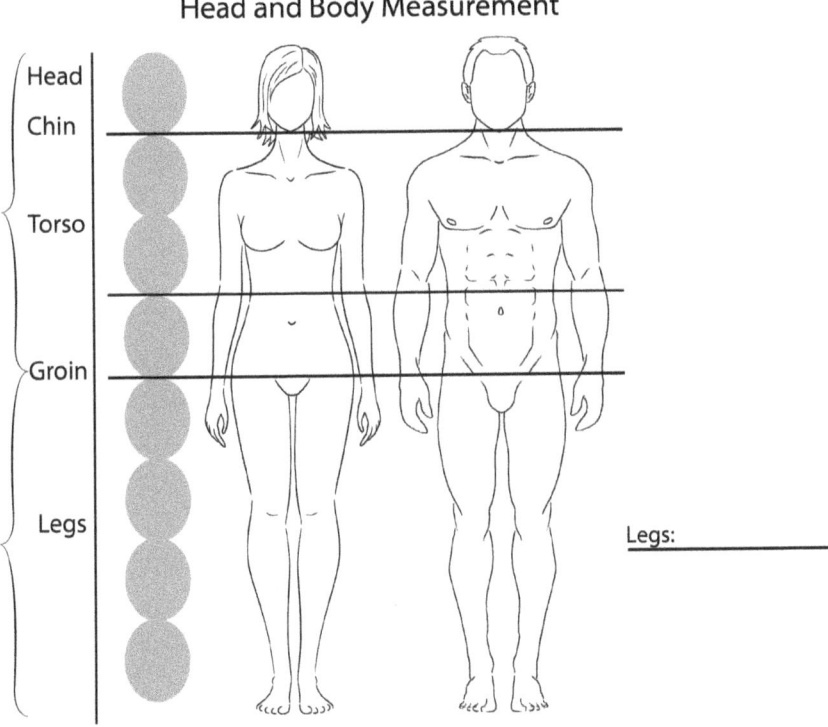

Figure 7.22

Most women want longer legs.

Check out these tips to lengthen (or shorten) the appearance of your legs:

- If you don't mind the discomfort, wearing heels is the easiest and fastest way to have long-looking legs. Of course, flats will do the opposite.
- Shoes the same color as your legs will extend their length, while a contrasting color will shorten them. Remember that

nude shoes are different colors for each of us; you could have a golden or honey appearance, pale pink, tan, brown, or black
- Pointed toes add to the appearance of length.
- When wearing skirts and dresses, showing your feet and ankles in your shoes will lengthen the appearance of your legs, and ankle straps and booties will shorten them.
- Depending on your modesty level, age, and occasion, showing more of your legs in dresses, skirts, and shorts above the knee will lengthen their appearance.

See Figure 7.23 to see these principles in action.

These are some additional easy tweaks to elongate your legs:

- Consider the break of your slacks. A shorter break, like a Capri or ankle-length pair of pants, will shorten your legs, while a more extended cut will lengthen your legs.
- Wearing shoes in the predominant color on your bottom half is also lengthening. If you have navy slacks, wear navy shoes, tan slacks with tan shoes, and so on.
- Short jackets, especially a cropped or bolero style, will further extend your bottom half (Figure 7.24).

Here are a couple of other ideas:

- As noted, a high-waisted pair of jeans or paper bag-style pants will create the illusion of long legs, whereas low-rise pants can shorten them. Pants with vertical lines are slimming and elongating, while patterns and horizontal lines can shorten the look.
- For those special nights out, consider skirts and dresses with high slits or asymmetric hems to lengthen your legs (Figure 7.25).

Balancing Act: Styling Your Body's Unique Proportions

Figure 7.23

Figure 7.24

Figure 7.25

Are you a man with longer legs?

Long legs is not a gender-specific issue. Many men have long torsos or torsos that are shorter than they wish, and they want to create the illusion of longer legs. Unlike women, you can't put on four-inch stilettos to instantly increase your height (unless you're a famous rock star, which, for our purposes, I am assuming you're not). But you can find shoes and boots with a slight heel. The break of your pant legs can be as helpful if you want longer legs. Start with slacks and pants with a more extended break. The shorter the break, the shorter your legs will appear. Figure 7.26 illustrates the difference in the break of your pants.

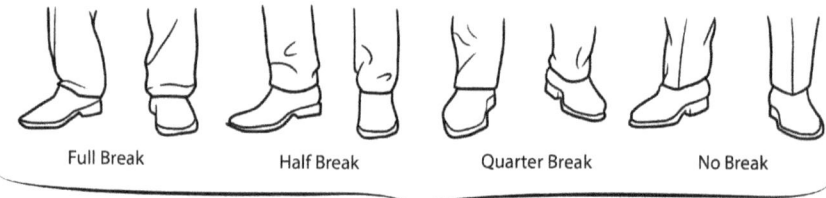

Full Break — Half Break — Quarter Break — No Break

Figure 7.26

Some other things for men to consider to lengthen their legs:

- Make sure your shoes match the color of your pants; the more color and tone variation, the shorter you appear. I love the look of colorful fancy socks, but they do interrupt the clean line achieved when wearing socks, shoes, and slacks of the same color (Figure 7.27).
- Tuck in shirts and sweaters.
- Untucked shirts, like T-shirts, should stay short, no longer than your hip bone.
- Belts should be the same color as your pants (Figure 7.28).

Balancing Act: Styling Your Body's Unique Proportions

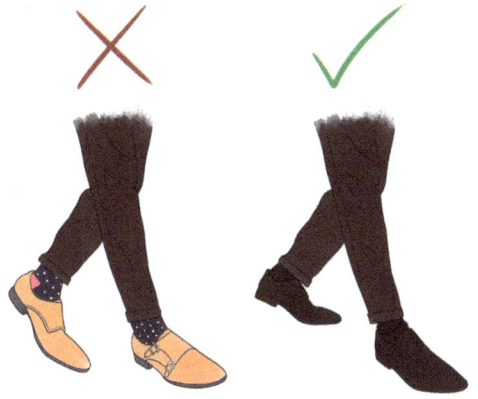

Figure 7.27

Figure 7.28

Understanding how to dress their unique body proportions has helped many clients. In particular, Naomi comes to mind. She is a fantastic person, full of energy, hardworking, intelligent, and personable. Yet before we met, she had spent most of her life trying to conceal perceived flaws in her personality and appearance—things only she saw in herself. She felt her personality was so big that it was overwhelming, and she often hid in her clothing to quiet her enthusiasm.

As we worked together, she learned to stop concealing her strengths and to match her outer persona to her inner confidence. Take a look at Figure 7.29 to see her before-and-after pictures.

Now look closely at Figure 7.30, and you will see how she applied the principles of body proportions. She said that simply adjusting her waistline and shirt length made her look and feel leaner and taller without losing a pound.

Naomi went on to create thriving organizations, run for office, and manage a significant initiative to reduce homelessness in her community. Did all this come from simply learning to dress her body and brand? Of course not. She was already a success when we met. But armed with confidence and a personal style to match, she is now unstoppable.

It's time to update your Ultimate Style Blueprint Summary Sheet with the details of your body proportions and which items you will choose to wear and avoid based on what you learned.

Balancing Act: Styling Your Body's Unique Proportions

Before   After

Figure 7.29

Figure 7.30

Chapter 8

ELEVATING YOUR LOOK WITH COLOR

I found I could say things with colors that I couldn't say in any other way—things I had no words for.

—*Georgia O'Keeffe*

Color theory is fascinating and complex. During your early education, you were likely introduced to colors and how to mix them and potentially the color wheel. At the college level, fine arts students spend significant time and coursework on color theory and its application to understand it fully.

The color wheel is a graphical depiction of color theory representing the relationship between primary, secondary, tertiary, adjacent, and complementary colors that was introduced to the world by Sir Isaac Newton in the seventeenth century. How we apply these principles today has changed and adapted to technology, but the principles have remained the same for all these years. Figure 8.0 shows Goethe's color wheel from the early nineteenth century.[1]

YOUR ULTIMATE STYLE BLUEPRINT

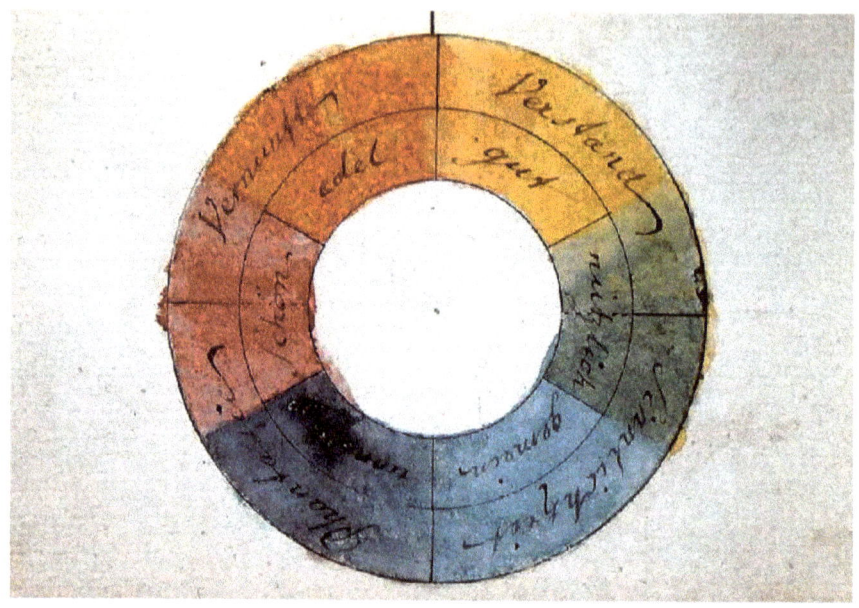

Figure 8.0

Color is essential for showcasing your best features and personality in fashion and dressing. When you walk into a clothing store, you will immediately see the trending colors and specific designer palettes for their current lines; you will either be drawn to or away from the colors on display.

I bet you have favorite colors and colors you know look good on you. I'm sure you have heard people say, "Wow, you look amazing in that color," or "That color makes your eyes pop." You have also seen the impact of particular colors on other people and how they can make a statement and enhance an individual's attractiveness. This doesn't occur by accident. We look our best in specific colors, tones, and shades when they harmonize with our natural palette, particularly when they highlight our eyes and other features.

COLOR THEORY AND TEMPERATURE

This chapter will give you an elementary review of color theory and how it applies to fashion. You will learn which colors are best for you and how to create stunning outfits by leveraging the same techniques artists use to create beautiful, interesting, and compelling works of art.

All you have to know is your palette and match that to the tones and shades in your clothing. This is best understood when following the concepts of color theory as illustrated by the color wheel. Let's take a closer look at a modern color wheel (Figure 8.1).

First, you will notice that it is divided into warm and cool colors. When thinking of warm and cool tones, the best analogy is a warm yellow sun compared to a cool blue ocean or sky. In art, pairing warm colors with warm colors and cool colors with cool colors creates a more harmonious, pleasing, and graceful outcome. The colors enhance and complement each other.

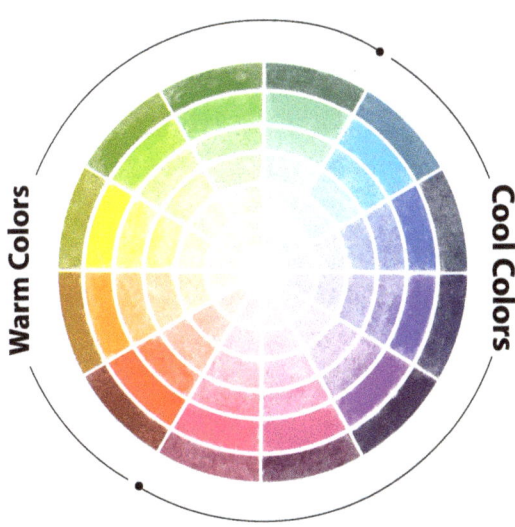

Figure 8.1

This concept also applies to humans. Most of us fall into one of these two categories; we each have either predominantly warm or cool undertones. This is complemented by our hair and eyes, which are also either warm or cool. It is less common, but you could be neutral, meaning you don't lean warm or cool, and many warm and cool colors look equally good on you.

Understanding your color temperature is where we start to determine which colors are most flattering on you. These questions will help you address that issue:

- **What color are your veins?** Our veins vary due to how light interacts with our skin and blood, how thick or thin our skin is, and how much melatonin is present. If your veins appear blue or purple, you likely have cool undertones. If they appear green or yellow, you likely have warm undertones.
- **What colors are in your undertones?** You probably have cool coloring if your skin is fair with pink or rosy undertones or medium to dark with slightly pink or blue undertones. On the other hand, if your skin is fair with yellow or golden undertones or darker with golden or orange undertones, you are likely to have warm coloring.
- **Do you tan?** You likely have warm coloring if you tan easily and your skin turns golden or brown. On the other hand, if you burn easily and your skin turns pink or red, you probably have cool coloring.
- **What looks good on you?** Do warm, earthy colors like red, orange, and yellow make you look radiant, or sallow or jaundiced? What about cool-colored jewel tones like ruby, sapphire, emerald, and amethyst? Do they bring you to life or overpower you and make you look ashy?
- **What color are your eyes?** Your eye color is more obvious. Blue and green are cool colors, brown is warm, and hazel is most often warm.

- **What color is your hair?** Golden blondes, golden brown, vibrant red, strawberry, copper, and orange hair are warm colors. Cool shades are ashy, gray, white, wheat, and black, with no golden hues, red, or warmth. If you aren't sure if your hair is warm or cool, ask your hairstylist. As a side note, this is the one feature you can change, and when you change your hair color from warm to cool or vice versa, you will likely change your natural color palette.

To confirm that you have figured out your color temperature, refer to the warm and cool palettes in Figure 8.4. Cut them out of the book and hold them to your face. Does one blend in beautifully and not the other? If so, you have your palette. I recommend you keep it with you when you shop. Also, start holding colors to your face, working next to a window with natural daylight. Try to wear only colors that bring out your best natural features, colors that are in your palette, and colors that blend nicely. This goes for all the clothes you wear, the color of jewelry metals (silver, gold, rose gold, gunmetal, etc.), gemstones and other materials, hats, scarves, ties, and nail polish.

If you have a warm complexion, does that mean you can't wear blue, green, purple, or pink? Absolutely not. Similarly, if you have a cool complexion, it doesn't mean you must avoid red, yellow, or orange. Each color has variations that can work for you. You'll just look best in hues that are mixed with your color temperature: blue-based for cool complexions or yellow-based for warm ones. Take a look at the primary colors in Figure 8.2 and notice what happens when blue or yellow is added to cool them down or warm them up. To the right, you see how the same color appears cooler, and to the left, a progressively warmer version.

I am often asked about black, white, and gray because these are missing from the color wheel and are the most common colors in fashion. The answer is, technically, they are not colors. They are considered absent of color. But in reality we consider them colors, and in practice they are cool colors and look best on people with pink and blue undertones. If you have a warm skin tone, these are not your best choices; I recommend brown and cream as a substitute. As you can see in Figure 8.3, if you add yellow to black, you get brown; if you add yellow to white, you get cream. These are the best warm versions of black and white.

Figure 8.2

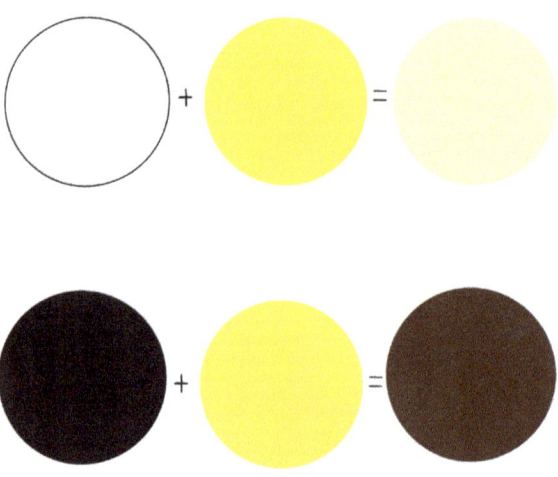

Figure 8.3

Elevating Your Look with Color

Figure 8.4

I hear you screaming from here, "But my whole wardrobe is black and gray!" This is very common. If you love the popular colors of black, white, and gray, don't let this discourage you; just be mindful of how they look on you. Ask yourself if you love them simply because you are habitually wearing them or if you honestly favor these colors. If the latter is the case, keep wearing them, but consider how you can layer other hues with them; for example, add a scarf, tie, jacket, or shirt in a color from your palette, maybe even the color of your eyes, a color you know flatters your features. Another idea is to choose lower necklines when wearing black, white, and gray so these colors are not right next to your face. This means a V-neck sweater or shirt with an open neckline for men. Ladies, you have more options for lower-cut tops and dresses.

COLOR CONTRAST LEVELS

Another thing to consider regarding wearing color is your natural contrast level, the depth and variance between your skin, hair, eyes, lips, and teeth. Then match your clothing to your natural contrast level. To understand this, rate your features on a very light to very dark scale. Go to a mirror and fill in the chart in Figure 8.5.

Feature	Very Light	Light	Medium	Dark	Very Dark
Skin					
Hair					
Irises					
Whites of Eyes					
Lips					
Teeth					

Figure 8.5

YOUR ULTIMATE STYLE BLUEPRINT

This is what the chart determines:

- You are considered low in contrast values if you mostly checked things as light, medium, or dark, with slight variation. For example, you have light hair, skin, lips, and irises; you checked things in one column.
- You are high contrast if you are in columns that run the gamut, such as light skin, dark hair, dark irises, bright white teeth, and dark red lips.
- You are medium contrast if you checked off a few columns near one another. For example, you have light brown skin, dark hair, dark eyes, medium lips, white teeth, and a light shade for the whites of your eyes. See Figure 8.6 for examples of low-, medium-, and high-contrast (left to right) skin tones.

Figure 8.6

Elevating Your Look with Color

What to do with this information? I recommend you dress in a way that matches your natural contrast level. Otherwise, your clothing may pull attention away from your face and to your clothing or another part of your body. This is especially true if your features are low contrast. We are unconsciously conditioned to look wherever we see the greatest intersection of contrast. So if you have little natural contrast in your facial features and a lot of contrast in your clothing, a viewer would be unconsciously directed toward your clothing and away from your face. Under most circumstances, this is the opposite of what you want. Instead, you want to attract others to look at your face.

Look at the patterns in the tops of the women in Figure 8.6 and notice how the contrast levels match their natural contrast levels. Can you imagine the low-contrast women with high-contrast clothing and how that could pull attention away from their faces?

What do you do if you have a big personality, want to be bright and festive, or are drawn to dramatic explosions of color, yet your features are of low contrast? In this case, consider adding more contrast to your natural palette. For women, this can be accomplished with makeup; consider darkening your eyebrows, wearing heavy eyeliner, mascara, eye shadow, and deeper lipstick shades. If you want this to be a more permanent solution, consider dyeing your hair to a dark and more vibrant color. Men can do this too; there's no reason you can't dye your hair to achieve an appearance that energizes you. If you wear glasses, consider a pair of shades that are chunky, stylish, and rich in color. Finally, whitening your teeth can help some; my recommendation is that your teeth match the whiteness of your eyes. If you have bright whites in your eyes and not in your teeth, teeth whitening might be a treatment you would like to consider.

If you already have a high-contrast complexion, you are freer to wear various shades of color. You can wear brighter hues if you feel outgoing and enthusiastic. If you want to be quieter or let someone else rule the roost that day, you can simply soften your color choices.

Give it a try. Go to your closet and look at your clothes, especially those you wear close to your face. Do they match your natural contrast level? Try the blink test when you get dressed. Stand in front of a full-length mirror, close your eyes, and then open them. What do you notice first—your face or your clothing? Are you drawn to a part of your body you want to emphasize or to conceal? Remember, it is most important to dress in a way that communicates your personality and brand. When people show up in ways that are inconsistent with who they are, it can be psychologically jarring, making them seem inconsistent and untrustworthy. Be authentic and consistent with the message you send through your appearance. Prioritize dressing in a way that communicates who you are, including the brightness or subtlety of your clothing's contrast level.

PSYCHOLOGY OF COLOR

You also should pay attention to the psychology of color because colors and shades of colors significantly impact our emotions, thoughts, and behaviors. If you're curious about specific colors, consider this:

- **Red** is an action color. It gives us energy, makes us move faster, and is associated with passion, danger, aggression, and anger.
- **Orange** represents enthusiasm, warmth, and playfulness; on the other hand, it also signals caution and warning.
- **Yellow** makes us feel happy and is full of sunshine and warmth. However, it can also be attention-grabbing and irritating.
- **Green** is often associated with nature, growth, balance, jealousy, envy, calmness, relaxation, and well-being.
- **Blue** is calming and relaxing; it connotes stability and trustworthiness. It can also be seen as cold and unemotional.
- **Purple** conjures mystery and spirituality and is often associated

Elevating Your Look with Color

with royalty and luxury. It has also been shown to promote creativity and imagination. In some cultures, dark purple is associated with death and mourning.
- **Black** is a powerful color associated with mystery, sophistication, and elegance. However, it can also be associated with depression, mourning, and intimidation. Black has also been shown to create a sense of seriousness and importance.
- **White** is often associated with purity, clarity, and simplicity. It is considered both modern and cold or even sterile and at the same time has been shown to promote openness and clarity.

Clearly, the same color can have multiple messages. Pay attention to the colors around you, think about how they make you feel, and consider what you want to communicate with your choice of colors.

The resonance of color is also a factor in the contrast level and how well these variations blend with our natural features. A color resonance is created by taking a base color, often called the hue, and adding a tone or additive to it: black, white, gray, brown, water, or the complementary color. Take a look at the various resonances in the color wheels shown in Figure 8.7. Hold them up to your face. You should find that one or two look especially good on you.

As with base colors, the resonance of colors has a unique psychological impact:

- Saturated colors are associated with bold, dramatic, exhilarating, high-energy emotions.
- Shaded colors are serious, profound, and mysterious.
- Toasted colors are warm, mellow, and luscious.
- Tinted colors are light-hearted, innocent, and sweet.
- Muted colors are soft, gentle, and subtle.
- Washed colors are similar to muted colors and provoke soft, lovely, demure, and quiet feelings.

YOUR ULTIMATE STYLE BLUEPRINT

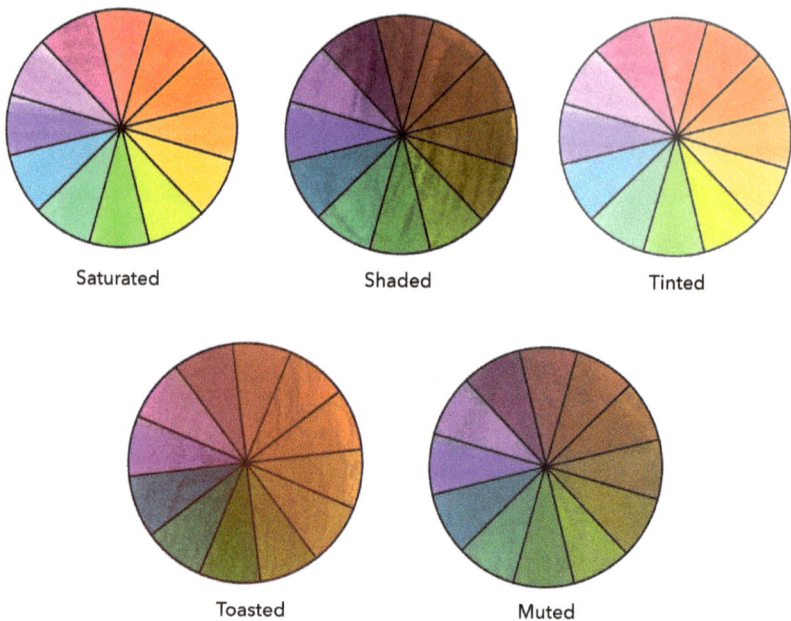

Figure 8.7

Knowing your color temperature (warm or cool) and your best resonance(s) of color, you should better understand the most flattering colors to wear, especially near your face.

Check out your closet and ask yourself what picture the color, or lack thereof, represents. Are the colors you identified for your palette hanging there? Do you see a wave of bright and cheery colors? Is there variety? Or do you see a sea of black and gray? Let this direct some next steps regarding items you want to add and potentially remove from your current wardrobe.

Determining a color palette that compliments your skin, hair, eyes, and personality will set you apart from most people. However, you can take it even further. When artists paint with color, they know how to combine colors to make a statement. That statement may be bold or soft but is always aesthetically pleasing. You can learn to think like an artist

Elevating Your Look with Color

and do the same as you are putting your outfits together, knowing how to mix and match colors in each ensemble you wear.

Looking around, you will see that most people play it safe, staying in black, gray, and white. You will also see other solids like navy blue, camel, brown, or burgundy. Brave dressers might add an article of clothing in a print and then match the rest of their outfit to the colors in that print. It's a good first step. Experiment with adding color and working with the colors each article of clothing provides. However, also consider using basic color theory to create unique color combinations. To understand this, look at the color wheel one last time, as shown in Figure 8.8. These harmonious color combinations are called color schemes: complementary, analogous, triadic, split complementary, and tetradic. Monochromatic is also a color scheme and was previously covered (see Chapter 7).

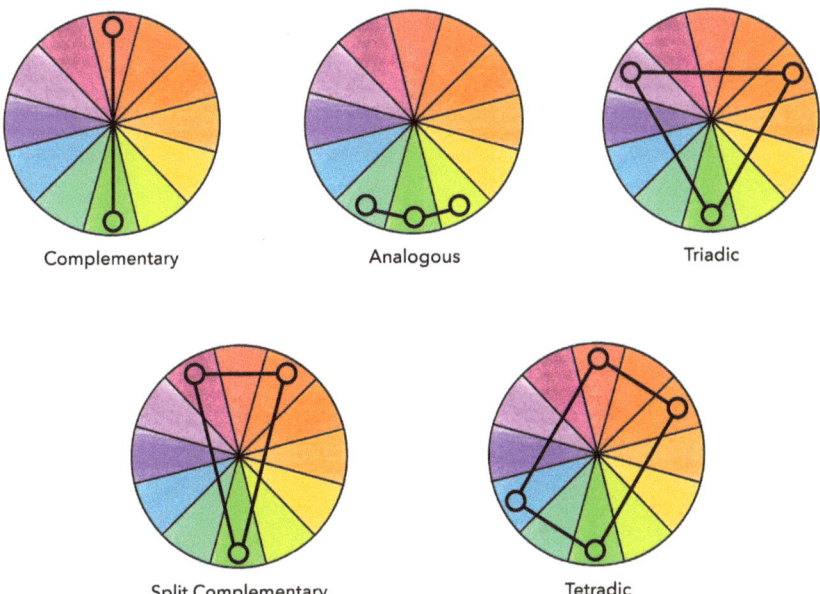

Figure 8.8

Buy solids and use color theory to mix and match wardrobe items. Consider layering pieces like camisoles or T-shirts in many colors, using these color schemes as your guide. Add pops of color with an accessory such as a bag, tie, jewelry, scarf, or shoes. Start by moving away from all black or gray if that is your comfort zone.

Monochromatic, analogous (colors next to each other on the color wheel), and complementary (colors across one another on the color wheel) colors are easy to envision and a great place to start your creative journey.

Most importantly, have fun with it. Consider your brand, natural contrast level, and color palette. Start to notice others. Are they dull or exciting in their use of colors? Is what they are wearing flattering or unappealing? The next time you go to a social event, notice the room and how attractive (or not) people who incorporate (or lack) color in their clothing appear.

My client Vanessa is a perfect example of someone who transformed her self-confidence and sense of style with the use of color. Vanessa's weight yo-yoed for much of her life, leaving her with a closet of ill-fitting clothes. This impacted her self-confidence. When we started working together, she was in a bit of a crisis. Her company was downsizing, and she and all the other HR department directors were asked to reapply for their jobs. The company would use this to determine who to keep and who to let go. She knew her peers well and knew the competition was tight. She needed to show up for the interviews at her best, exuding self-confidence.

She discovered her Ultimate Style Blueprint and found clothes that fit her perfectly. But the real transformation occurred when she wore bright colors matching her enthusiastic, infectious personality.

I'm happy to report she walked into the job interviews self-assured and saved her job! She found that the color green, especially, gave her energy. Today, she incorporates that color into everything she wears. Not too long ago, she told me someone at work challenged her not to wear green. She tried it for a week and reported back that she felt naked and listless, like something was off.

Elevating Your Look with Color

I'm not suggesting you find one color as a superpower. But I think you will discover that specific colors and color schemes will brighten your mood, build your self-confidence, and attract people to you. Take a look at Vanessa's before-and-after photos (Figure 8.9). Consider making some before-and-after pictures of your own.

How will you use color and color contrast as you shop and put outfits together? Return to your Ultimate Style Blueprint Summary Sheet and make notes to keep your goals around color readily accessible.

Figure 8.9

Chapter 9

ARTISTRY IN DETAIL: LINE, SCALE, TEXTURE, AND PATTERN

The details are not the details. They make the design.
—Charles Eames

The recent chapters covered the most impactful art and design elements: shape, proportion, and color. In this chapter, you will learn about additional subtle art concepts that will continue to enhance and empower you to stand out with style. As they say, "the devil is in the details."

LINE

Line is a foundational element of art used to convey a wide range of ideas and emotions. It is also a valuable tool in the art of fashion and style. In Chapter 7, you saw how vertical lines can elongate the body and create a slimming effect, while horizontal stripes can make the body appear wider. Diagonal lines can add interest and movement to an outfit, while curved lines can soften harsh angles and create a more feminine look.

Another consideration of line in fashion relates to your body's silhouette. This differs from its shape, as we previously discussed. Your lines may be soft, muscular, lean, or a combination of the three, commonly classified as ectomorph, mesomorph, or endomorph body types. Take a look at Figure 9.0. Understanding this can help you determine which fabrics most complement your body in terms of the texture and the drape of the material.

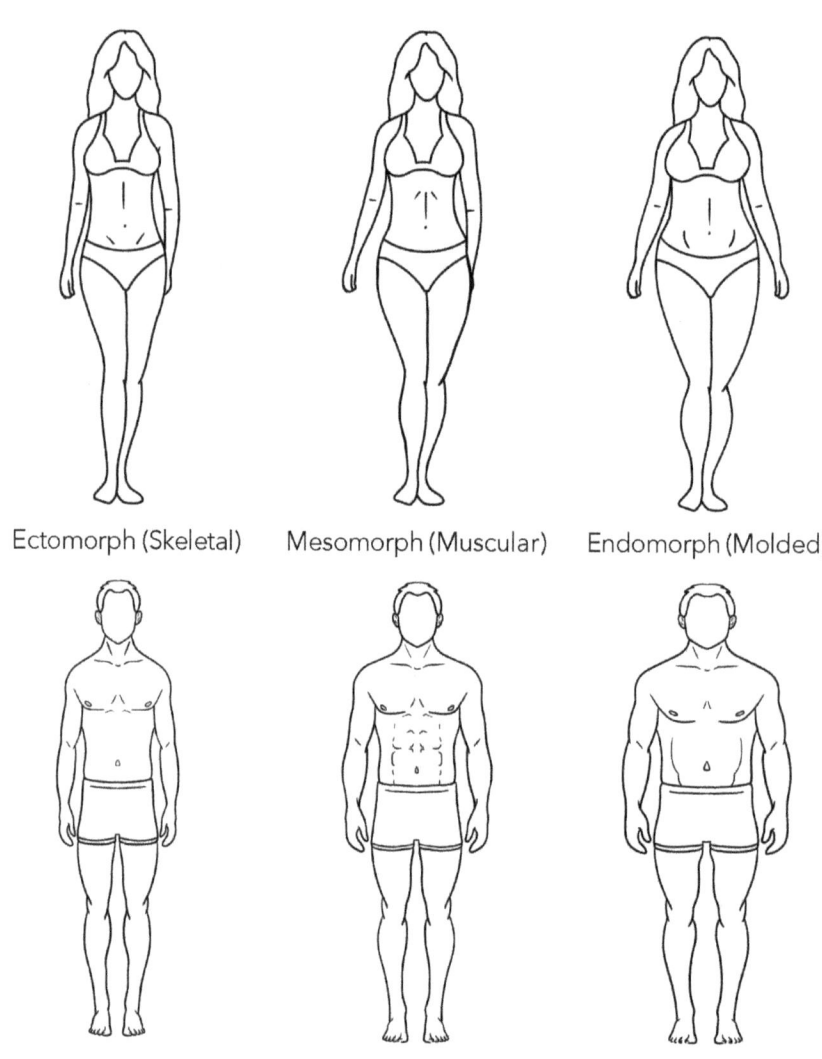

Figure 9.0

Artistry in Detail: Line, Scale, Texture, and Pattern

Ectomorph. You likely have an ectomorph body type if you are very thin and have visible collar bones and hip bones. Fabrics with some texture can create the illusion of depth and fullness in this body type. Similarly, materials with some weight or structure, such as denim or wool, can be flattering. These fabrics hang more fluidly and can add visual weight to the body. Conversely, very lightweight or clingy materials, such as silk or jersey, can sometimes emphasize a thin frame, potentially making you look bony. That's not to say that these fabrics should be avoided altogether, but it's important to consider how they will drape and fit you. Take a look at Figure 9.1 for an example.

Figure 9.1

Mesomorph. If you have a muscular build, you are likely a mesomorph. Your best fabrics support muscle tone and provide stretch and flexibility for ease of movement. Synthetic materials, such as nylon and polyester, are good choices, as is modal, a fabric similar to rayon known for its softness, breathability, and stretch. Consider cotton blends with spandex, which can provide a comfortable fit with some stretch, making it easier to move and bend while showing off that beautiful, tight body. Figure 9.2 shows this type.

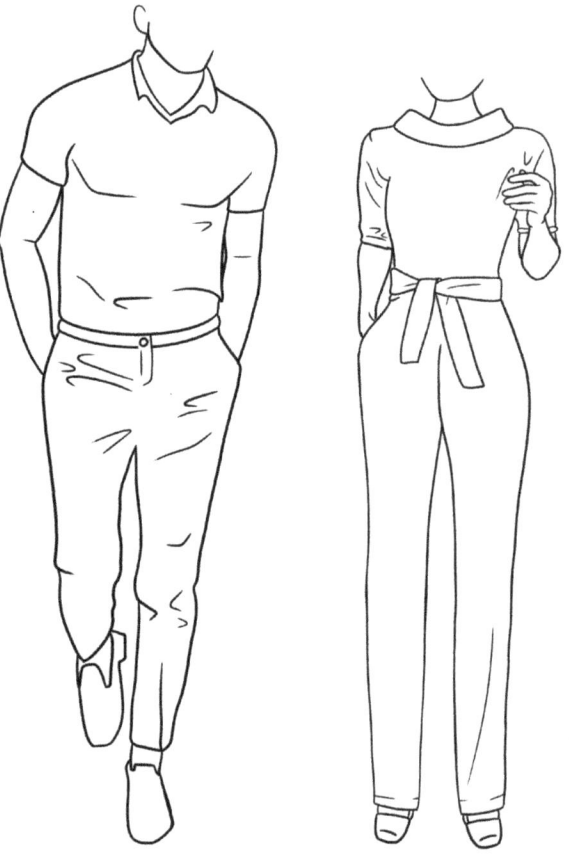

Figure 9.2

Artistry in Detail: Line, Scale, Texture, and Pattern

Endomorph. You are likely an endomorph if your body is soft to the touch. If this sounds like you, it does not mean you are overweight; in fact, most women fall into this category. Fabrics with a bit of structure are flattering. Denim, tweed, Ponte (a double knit), and other structured knits can add definition and enhance your silhouette. Garments with movement also work well with this body type. Check out Figure 9.3 for an example of this look.

Figure 9.3

It is common to be more than one of these body types. For example, you might have strong legs and glutes and a thin torso, making you a mesomorph on the bottom and an ectomorph on the top. Or you could be thin on top, with a soft belly, hips, thighs, or bottom: ectomorph and endomorph. Some men find that they have extra weight around their middle with a solid chest and legs: mesomorph and endomorph.

No matter which build or line makes up your body constitution, the fit of your clothing is critical. The muscular body can handle the tightest fit, but even in that case, too tight is still too tight. Think of *Goldilocks and the Three Bears*: You want fabrics that are "just right," materials that support your natural lines.

SCALE

Scale, as an aspect of art, refers to the relative size of objects or figures in relation to one another within a design or to the viewer. Scale can emphasize certain elements, create impact or drama, or convey a mood or feeling. Large-scale objects or figures can create a feeling of power or dominance, while small-scale objects or figures can create a sense of vulnerability or insignificance.

We can apply this concept to fashion and how we dress by considering how the size and scale of different elements and patterns in an outfit relate to each other and, more importantly, to us. Scale can create a balanced and harmonious look or add visual interest and drama to your look.

Matching your clothing and accessories to your natural scale is best. For example, if you have a slight build, small-scale designs, buttons, zippers, facings, cuffs, and accessories are most flattering. Conversely, bulky, boxy styles, large designs, and accessories will overwhelm your frame and overshadow you. The opposite is true for larger-scale individuals. If you choose small prints, buttons, accessories, and so on, these items will be too small, making you appear large and awkward by contrast.

Unfortunately, too many designers apply the same design elements regardless of the scale of the individual. Instead, we need styles for petite

Artistry in Detail: Line, Scale, Texture, and Pattern

versus curvy women and small and trim versus big and tall men. This also goes for the scale of your shoes. Women, in particular, should consider whether they have thin, average, or large athletic calves and ankles. The chunky heels and combat boots that have been on trend for several years can almost comically overwhelm a thin woman. Conversely, a larger-scale woman in kitten heels may appear as though she will topple over at any moment. Men have the same issue to consider, but it isn't as challenging because their selection of shoe styles is much narrower.

Recently, I was helping my college-age son shop for gym clothing. He is thin and tall, and no matter how hard he works out, his legs will always be genetically thin for his frame. While shopping with me, he saw how gym shorts that were a bit shorter and narrower made a big difference. The longer and wider shorts just emphasized the narrowness of his legs.

So when it comes to scale, think about your body and consider the size and design of the items you wear. Do they emphasize something you prefer to minimize, or do they complement your strengths?

See Figures 9.4 and 9.5 for examples of how to adjust the scale of your accessories, as well as prints and patterns, to match your physical scale.

You can also take size into account when combining outfits, mixing different sizes of prints or design elements to create visual balance, interest, or drama.

YOUR ULTIMATE STYLE BLUEPRINT

Figure 9.4

Figure 9.5

Artistry in Detail: Line, Scale, Texture, and Pattern

TEXTURE

As with painting or sculpture, texture in fashion creates depth, contrast, and intrigue. It can evoke emotions, convey a sense of luxury or simplicity, and subtly communicate aspects of your personality. The interplay of different fabrics—from the softness of cashmere to the roughness of denim or the sleekness of satin to the richness of velvet—can transform an outfit.

Fabrics like silk, satin, and polished cotton are sleek and sophisticated. Soft textures like cashmere, velvet, or faux fur are plush and evoke a sense of luxury and coziness. Conversely, materials like wool, tweed, and denim have a more tactile quality and project a more casual feel. Shiny textures like sequins and metallics reflect light and create a glamorous effect.

Take a look at the fabrics you own and are drawn to and ask yourself what feelings they evoke. Is that consistent with your personal brand and the message you want to communicate about yourself?

When putting outfits together, you can stick to similar textures to project a consistent look and feel. However, I recommend combining different textures into one outfit to add depth and dimension. For example, pair a smooth silk top with tweed slacks or a leather jacket over a lace dress. I especially like to layer texture in a monochromatic look to add an extra feeling of sophistication and interest. Check out Figure 9.6 for some common textures that make different statements. Considering texture as you choose your wardrobe items will help you appear polished and intentional and take your outfits and style to a new level.

Figure 9.6

PATTERN

Patterns are used in art to create rhythm, movement, and harmony. In the world of fashion, patterns do more than just decorate; they tell stories, evoke emotions, and transform your silhouette. Whether it's the bold geometry of stripes, checks, or plaid, the timeless elegance of polka dots, or the exotic allure of animal prints, patterns bring life and movement to fabric.

These patterns convey unique messages and emotions:

Stripes. As well as being slimming and elongating, vertical stripes are often associated with formality and sophistication, especially when used in business attire, such as pinstripe suits. Horizontal stripes, on

Artistry in Detail: Line, Scale, Texture, and Pattern

the other hand, create a sense of width and stability. They typically have a more informal feel, commonly seen in nautical and casual wear. Diagonal stripes can suggest movement, adding a sense of energy. They are less formal than vertical stripes and can create a more playful or modern look.

Checks. There are different variations of checks used in fashion, most commonly projecting timeless elegance. The most popular checkered patterns are illustrated in Figure 9.7: gingham (top left), windowpane (top right), houndstooth (bottom left), and Prince of Wales (bottom right).

Figure 9.7

Plaid. Plaid is a variation of checks but typically more complex with intersecting lines and multiple colors. The most popular plaids are shown in Figure 9.8: tartan (top left), madras (top right), tattersall (bottom left), and lumberjack or buffalo (bottom right). Each has it's own look and feel and significance. Tartan plaids come from Scotland and are associated with warmth and comfort. Madras is lightweight and colorful and communicates a casual, preppy style. The tattersall has equestrian roots and has a refined and classic feel. The lumberjack, also called buffalo plaid with the iconic black-and-red check pattern, is commonly seen in flannel shirts and known for durable, warm clothing that is suitable for working outdoors in cold conditions.

YOUR ULTIMATE STYLE BLUEPRINT

Figure 9.8

Polka Dots. Polka dots can range from small and subtle to large and bold. They are often associated with playfulness, femininity, and a retro or vintage aesthetic. Smaller dots tend to be more sophisticated and delicate, while larger dots are bolder and more whimsical.

Floral Patterns. Floral patterns can vary widely in style, from delicate and romantic to bold and tropical. Although florals conjure up feelings of femininity, they are growing in popularity for men's attire and add an approachable and modern feeling to everything from slacks to shirts and jackets.

Animal Prints. Patterns like leopard, zebra, or snakeskin evoke exoticism, boldness, and a sense of adventure. Animal prints are often used to make a statement and convey confidence, edginess, and a touch of sex appeal.

Paisley. This teardrop-shaped pattern has origins in Persian and Indian designs. Once associated with bohemian, artistic, and exotic styles, paisley patterns have become mainstream and can add a subtle touch of sophistication to a tie or scarf or more drama in bolder colors and larger palettes, such as a jacket or pair of pants.

Geometric Patterns. Patterns, such as squares, triangles, and abstract shapes, can convey modernity, structure, and a sense of order. They are often associated with contemporary, urban styles and can range from minimalist designs to complex, intricate arrangements.

REPEATING PATTERNS AND RELATEDNESS

Repeating patterns are a common technique where identical or similar elements, such as shapes, lines, or colors, repeat at regular intervals, creating texture, depth, and a sense of movement across a space. They can be found in wallpaper designs, textiles, and architectural details and are frequently used in abstract and decorative art. Repeating patterns are also used in clothing. For example, the simple flow of floral prints or polka dots can evoke a sense of romanticism and femininity, while bold checks or plaid designs offer a stronger structured appearance, and repetitive geometric shapes suggest modernity and creativity.

Relatedness, another art concept, refers to the sense of connection or coherence between different elements. It doesn't necessarily involve identical repetition. Instead, relatedness can be achieved through the use of similar colors or shapes. Our brains are miraculously hardwired to spot patterns and similarities. When we see a color or shape, our unconscious seeks to find that color or shape elsewhere. This instinct goes back to our early days as humans when recognizing patterns could mean the difference between danger and safety. So when we see repeating patterns in fashion or design, it creates a sense of harmony and balance. This principle is widely used to direct a viewers' eye in art, architecture, interior design, and fashion. Take a look at Figure 9.9 to see a home design using these concepts and Figure 9.10, where I applied the same principles to a few Success thru Style avatars.

YOUR ULTIMATE STYLE BLUEPRINT

Figure 9.9

Figure 9.10

Artistry in Detail: Line, Scale, Texture, and Pattern

As you can see, mastering the subtler aspects of style—like line, scale, texture, and pattern—can significantly elevate your personal presentation. These elements are more than mere details; they are powerful tools that allow you to express your individuality, enhance your natural features, and convey the right message about who you are. Whether you're choosing fabrics that complement your body type, selecting patterns that tell a story, or combining textures to add depth to your look, it's all about being intentional and thoughtful with your choices.

It's time to update your Ultimate Style Blueprint Summary Sheet with notes on how you will incorporate Line, Scale, Texture and Pattern into your wardrobe.

Chapter 10

ENHANCING YOUR FEATURES: FACE SHAPES AND MAKEUP

The face is a picture of the mind with the eyes as its interpreter.
—*Marcus Tullius Cicero*

Up to this point, in addition to personal branding, we have focused on how to dress your body. We have only touched on how this will bring attention to your face. But isn't your face the most important feature? It is at the heart of your interaction with others. It's often what people see first, whether from your headshot, a video call, or in person. You sit across the table or shake someone's hand, look into their eyes, and begin a conversation. The next two chapters are about your face and hair and how to bring attention to your face and present it at its best.

Have you ever considered the shape of your face? If not, you're not unique; this is typically a new concept for most clients. But your face is a definite shape, and you've read enough to know that's important information.

Your face is likely round, oval, oblong, rectangular, square, heart, or diamond shaped. Occasionally, someone is an outlier with a different shape, but that is rare. Generally, for those seeking a masculine appearance, a square shape with a chiseled jawline is deemed most desirable, whereas a softer jawline, specifically an oval shape, is considered ideal for women.

As I have said before, not only do beauty standards and social norms change, but our personal preferences are unique. For example, I favor the heart- or diamond-shaped face in women because I love the high cheekbones. What about you? I challenge you to notice not only your face shape but that of others. What appeals to you and why? All face shapes are attractive. Do a quick search online of the various face shapes, and you will see that those we consider classically beautiful and handsome have all the shapes.

DETERMINING FACE SHAPE

To figure out your face shape:

- Stand in front of a well-lit mirror with your hair pulled back and away to see your entire face.
- Examine the width and length of your face.
- Look at the prominent features, like your forehead, cheekbones, jawline, and chin.
- Check out Figure 10.0 for examples of women's face shapes and 10.1 for men's. Compare the width and length of your face to the different face shapes pictured.

Consider these brief descriptions of the different face shapes:

- **A round face** is soft with curved lines. It is similar in width and length, with cheekbones at the widest part of the face. The jawline is curved compared to a square face, which is angular.
- **An oval face** has balanced proportions, with the length slightly longer than the width, and the forehead and jawline are gently rounded.
- **A square face** is similar to a round face but has sharp lines, a strong, angular jawline, and a broad forehead. It is also similar in width and length.
- **A rectangle face,** more common than a square shape in men, is a longer version of the square face.

Enhancing Your Features: Face Shapes and Makeup

- **An oblong face** is long and narrow. Typically, the cheekbones in this shape are not very prominent.
- **A heart-shaped face** has prominent cheekbones, a broad forehead, and a narrow chin.
- **A diamond-shaped face** has a narrow forehead and chin with cheekbones at the widest part of the face.

Figure 10.0

If you aren't sure which shape you have, try drawing it in a mirror. It's messy, but I've found this to work well. Grab something erasable, like lipstick or eyeliner. Look at yourself and trace the outline of your face. It should become clear.

YOUR ULTIMATE STYLE BLUEPRINT

Figure 10.1

Now that you have it, you might be asking, why does it matter? The answer is that it's incredible how many things your face shape can influence as you develop your personal style. It can significantly impact your appearance when you consider neckline shapes, makeup application, hairstyles (covered at length in the next chapter), facial hair, and accessories (detailed in Chapter 12), such as handbags, hats, jewelry, and eyewear.

FACE SHAPE AND NECKLINES

Starting with necklines, it's fascinating how simple choices can complement facial features. The first thing to consider is the concept of repeating patterns covered in the previous chapter. Repeating the shape of your face

Enhancing Your Features: Face Shapes and Makeup

with your neckline creates harmony. For example, wearing a V-neck top will gracefully echo your jaw and bring attention to your face if you have a diamond- or heart-shaped face.

Look at Figures 10.2 and 10.3 for illustrations of the most common types of necklines found in women's and men's fashion.

Figure 10.2

YOUR ULTIMATE STYLE BLUEPRINT

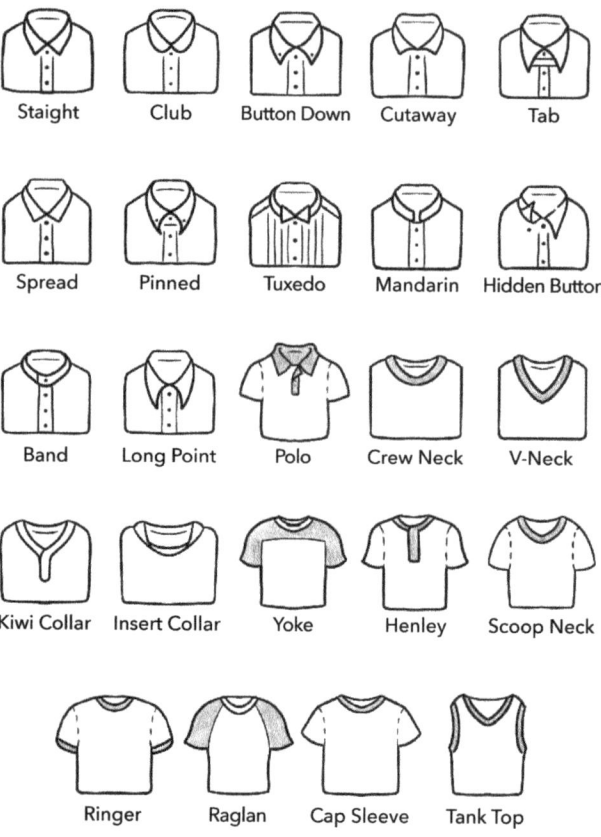

Figure 10.3

You will notice some are more curved, some create a V-shape, some are wide, and some are narrow. Repeating your face's shape with the neckline's opening will create harmony. Of course, this is not a hard and fast rule, meaning that if you're like me and have a square face, you're not limited only to wide square necklines and have to avoid scoops or V-shaped necklines. However, if I see a top I like that has a wide scoop or square neckline, I am more inclined to buy it. I know it will be more flattering on me than other choices.

In addition to repeating the pattern of your face shape, you can compensate for your natural shape, specifically trimming what is wide,

Enhancing Your Features: Face Shapes and Makeup

lengthening what is short, shortening what is long, and widening what is narrow. See Figure 10.4 and consider the following:

- To widen a narrow face, such as an oblong, wear necklines thinner than the broadest part of your face.
- To trim a wide face shape, such as a round or square, wear necklines wider than the broadest part of your face.
- To lengthen the appearance of your face, choose lower-cut necklines.
- To shorten a long face, wear high necklines.

Figure 10.4

Play around with it. Train your eye to see the impact of the various necklines you wear. The little things can make all the difference in how you look and feel about your appearance.

A note for men: Although the selections of necklines and collar styles are much narrower for you than for women, there are various collars, T-shirts, sweaters, and polo shirt styles to consider. The same concept of repeating patterns applies. However, most men focus more on their overall size and scale. For example, if you have a square, round, or broad face, a collar with the tips pointing down creates a vertical sightline for the eyes that is slimming and elongating. A spread collar will create a fuller look if you have a diamond-shaped, oblong, or tall face. Spread collars are wider and point away horizontally, which will help balance a longer face, making it look broader and more substantial. Refer back to Figure 10.3 for examples of men's shirts and collars.

Now would be a good time to update your Ultimate Style Blueprint Summary Sheet, noting your face shape and the necklines that best suit you.

SKIN CARE

When discussing faces, we can't ignore the topic of skin care. It is fundamental to our appearance, for both men and women. Your skin is the largest organ in your body. There are reasons to take care of it beyond just wanting to look your best. It is essential to your appearance and health.

I'm sure you think about skin care as a way to moisturize your skin and help it look clean, fresh, and youthful. However, a good skin care routine also helps maintain your skin's barrier function and protects you from damage caused by pollution, UV radiation, and free radicals. Moisturizers and other hydrating products can help improve the skin's overall health and function. Certain skin care ingredients can also provide therapeutic benefits. For example, products containing salicylic acid can help unclog pores and reduce acne breakouts, and products containing ceramides can

Enhancing Your Features: Face Shapes and Makeup

help improve the skin's barrier function in individuals with eczema or other inflammatory skin conditions. Of course, applying moisturizer with SPF can help shield against skin damage and cancer.

If you want to go deeper, some skin care products, such as serums and certain moisturizers, can affect the dermis layer where collagen, elastin, and other structural components reside. Products containing ingredients like retinoids, vitamin C, and peptides can help stimulate collagen production and improve your skin's overall health and appearance. Finally, some skin care treatments, such as chemical peels and laser resurfacing, can affect even deeper layers of the skin, including the subcutaneous tissue. These treatments are typically performed by a dermatologist or other trained professional and address specific skin concerns, such as deep wrinkles, scarring, or hyperpigmentation. There are many treatments you can consider, but at a basic level, we should all do the following daily:

- Cleanse in the morning and night to remove dirt, oil, and impurities from the skin.
- Tone after cleansing to balance the skin's pH, minimize the appearance of pores, and prepare the skin for the next steps of the routine.
- Exfoliate a few times weekly to remove dead skin cells from the skin's surface.
- Moisturize to hydrate and protect the skin.
- Treat as needed to target conditions such as acne, dark spots, or fine lines and wrinkles.

It is important to choose skin care products appropriate for your skin type and patch-test new products before using them on your face to avoid allergic reactions or other adverse effects. I once bought a new skin care product from a quality, all-natural brand and had an allergic reaction. My face turned bright red and blew up to the size of a pumpkin.

Skin care is just as important for men as it is for women. Men's skin tends to be thicker and oilier, making it more prone to breakouts and other skin conditions. A good skin care routine can help balance natural oils, reduce inflammation, and promote a clearer, more even complexion. Additionally, using a moisturizer after shaving can help prevent irritation, razor burn, and dryness.

Skin care products can be costly. My experience indicates that there isn't a correlation between price and results. The price has more to do with brand recognition and marketing; therefore, I recommend focusing on quality ingredients and the manufacturer's size. The larger the company, the more money it has for research and development and, therefore, the ability to offer the best products. Skin care products across the board are known to be overpriced, so spending some time comparing products should pay off.

MAKEUP

There are even more options to consider when evaluating makeup, which is a multibillion-dollar industry with countless products available. Both men and women of all ages use makeup, which continues to evolve with new trends and innovations.

Makeup has a rich history. It was invented by the ancient Egyptians when men and women wore it to enhance their appearance and social status. However, by the Middle Ages, it was worn solely by prostitutes and actors due to disapproval from the Catholic Church, which associated it with vanity and temptation. It came back into favor in the sixteenth century, particularly among the upper classes. In the nineteenth century, it became more widely available and continued to grow in popularity, evolving into what it is today.[1]

At present, women wear makeup more commonly; however, some men wear it to enhance their features, cover blemishes, or for special occasions like photo shoots, weddings, and performances. Who knows what the future holds? Recently, we have seen celebrities and public figures

Enhancing Your Features: Face Shapes and Makeup

openly share their experiences wearing makeup, which has helped to break down gender stereotypes and encourage more men to feel comfortable with it.

Whether you choose to wear makeup is a personal choice. Many people prefer a natural look and to avoid the expense and time associated with it. Others won't leave the house without it. My opinion: it is an invaluable tool. For most women, well-applied makeup adds to your appearance, enhancing features, concealing imperfections, and even restructuring the shape of your face, eyes, and lips. Most of my female clients gain confidence when they understand how to apply makeup: using the right tools, finding colors that work for them, and perfecting basic techniques.

If you need more confidence with makeup, want feedback on how current you look, or wish to gain some new techniques, makeup artists are readily available. Like most professionals, some are better than others. More than that, makeup is an art form, and you will want to ensure the artist's style is in sync with your goals. Most likely, you are looking for someone who can instruct you on everyday makeup techniques, not for a theatrical look or wedding day glamour. Here are some tips to help you find the right person:

- Ask people you know and trust for personal referrals and recommendations.
- Look online for well-rated resources.
- Have a discussion and check out their portfolio to make sure their style aligns with your goals.
- One caveat to consider: many makeup artists sell makeup. In this case, be sure they are making recommendations solely based on what is right for you, not to ring up makeup sales. On the other hand, if you are on a budget, many makeup professionals will offer you a complimentary makeover for a minimum makeup purchase.

In addition to makeup artists, online makeup videos are readily available and will teach you how to do it yourself. You can also get help at the makeup counter at local department stores or beauty superstores.

Even if you have been applying makeup for years, getting help from a professional periodically is useful. As we age, our faces change, and the techniques we used in the past often no longer work. New products hit the market, and the trends are constantly changing. Here are my recommendations for an everyday makeup routine:

- **Primer.** Just like painting a wall, the primer smooths your skin and prepares the surface of your face for the next step. Everything else applies and looks better after this step.
- **Foundation.** This is necessary, but less is more as we age. A thicker, cakier makeup can, unfortunately, emphasize wrinkles. A color-correcting (CC) cream or tinted moisturizer might provide the perfect coverage to help smooth out your skin and give it a youthful glow. Some lines like Bobbi Brown are designing new products with lots of moisture for the aging face. If you are still determining what brand or type of foundation you want, head to a department store or beauty superstore where you can discuss the options with a sales clerk and get samples to try. Matching the right color to your skin should be done in person and with natural light. Foundation is one of the most essential cosmetics you will wear as it smooths your skin and is applied to your entire face and under the chin.
- **Concealer.** An essential product in your cosmetics bag and one where quality ingredients matter. Apply concealer under your eyes to remove dark areas and anywhere else you want to cover up. Your eyes are your most important feature and where you want others to focus their attention. Brighten and lighten this area to help highlight your eyes.

Enhancing Your Features: Face Shapes and Makeup

- **Setting powder and spray.** These are especially useful for long, busy days. They reduce shine and create longevity for the other products you have applied.
- **Contouring and highlighting.** You can highlight and diminish specific areas by applying bronzer to create a shadow effect and highlighter to brighten a particular area. A typical application is to apply a highlighter to the cheekbones and bronzer just below; this emphasizes and pronounces the cheekbones. In addition, you can reduce an angular jaw or large forehead with a bronzer. Remember to highlight anything you want to accentuate and contour anything you wish to diminish. See Figure 10.5 for ways to contour and highlight to change and enhance your face shape.

Figure 10.5

- **Blush.** When contouring your cheekbones, you need very little blush. In this case, sparingly apply a blush color that complements your skin tone on the apple of your cheeks. Blush will help create a happy, youthful appearance.
- **Eye makeup.** Because eyes vary widely in shape and size, how we apply eye makeup differs significantly. Check out Figure 10.6 for the most common eye shapes.

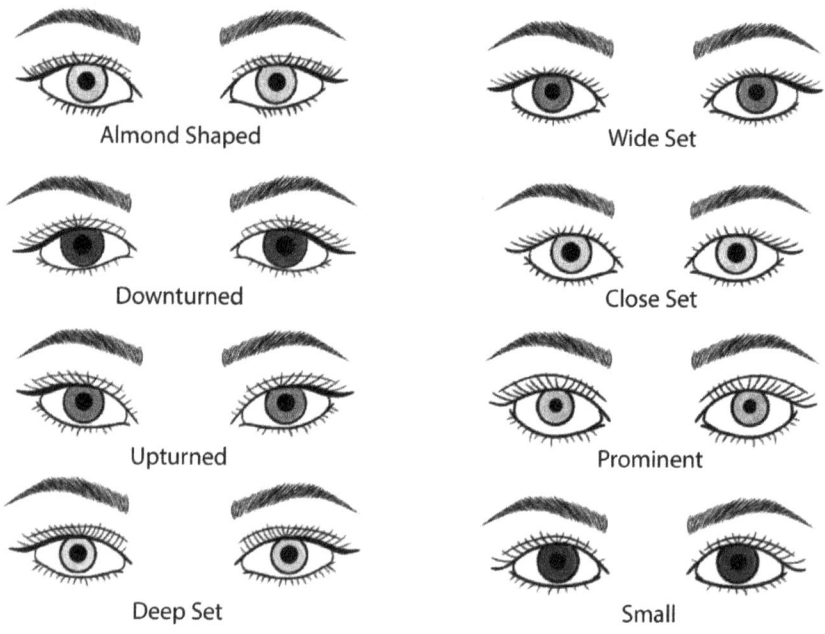

Figure 10.6

There are several eye products to consider. I recommend an eye primer, shades of eye shadow depending on your eye shape, eyeliner, and mascara. How you apply eye makeup again differs depending on your lifestyle and the image you wish to project. Do you want to focus on the dramatic, or are you more natural? Eye makeup changes with the season, the trends are highly volatile, and our eyes change with age. However, there are some things makeup professionals recommend based on the shape of your eyes:

Enhancing Your Features: Face Shapes and Makeup

- **Almond eyes**, also called standard eyes, are the most coveted eye shape; most application techniques suit them.
- **Wide-set eyes** are further apart than one eye's width. To bring them closer together, darken the inner corner of your eyes and shade over and upward. Apply eyeliner fully on the upper lid and mascara on all lashes.
- **Down-turned eyes** tilt down in the outer corners. To lift them, add color slightly along the bottom lash and brush up and over. Apply eyeliner on the upper lid and lift it slightly at the corner. Apply mascara to the upper lid.
- **Close-set eyes** are closer together than one eye's width. To widen them, apply dark shades on the outside and light shades on the inside of your eyes. Apply mascara and eyeliner to the outer corners.
- **Upturned eyes** are very similar to almond-shaped eyes. They have an oval shape and a natural upward lift at the outer edges. With upturned eyes, the lower lid tends to be more prominent, appearing much longer than the top lid. You may decide applying eyeliner to enhance the natural symmetry and shape of the eyes is desirable.
- **Prominent eyes** sit outside the eye socket, the opposite of deep-set eyes. If you prefer them to recede more, apply dark eye shadow close to the lash line, fading to lighter colors moving toward your brow. Avoid light colors on your lid. Apply eyeliner and mascara fully around the eye.
- **Deep-set eyes** sit deeper in the socket. To bring them forward, apply light color on the lids and blend from light to dark from the inner corner to the outside. Apply eyeliner and mascara fully.
- **Small eyes** can appear more prominent by adding a light shimmery color to the lid, a darker color in the crease, and a light color up to the brow. Also, a white pencil in the waterline of the eye can significantly enlarge their appearance.

Hooded eyes occur with age, and for these eyes, less is more. To reduce the hooding appearance, apply one shade, at least as dark as the crease. Apply eyeliner and mascara, especially to the corners, to lift.

Keep in mind that you can have more than one shape. For example, they can be hooded and downturned or small and close-set. If you aren't confident about applying eye makeup or it's been a while, I again recommend that you find a makeup professional who is a good fit for you and can teach you how to complement your natural beauty.

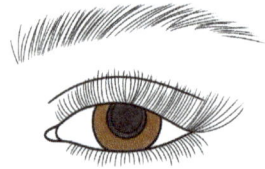 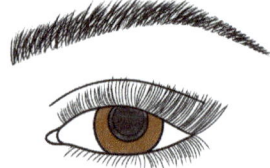

Figure 10.7

- **Eyebrows.** Shaping and filling in your brows is essential. Your eyebrows are the frame of your eyes, much the same way a picture is showcased inside a frame. The biggest mistake I see is brows that need to be darker and lengthened. If this is new, I recommend you find a professional to wax and shape them. You also may want to work with a professional makeup artist. Seeing yourself with this enhancement may

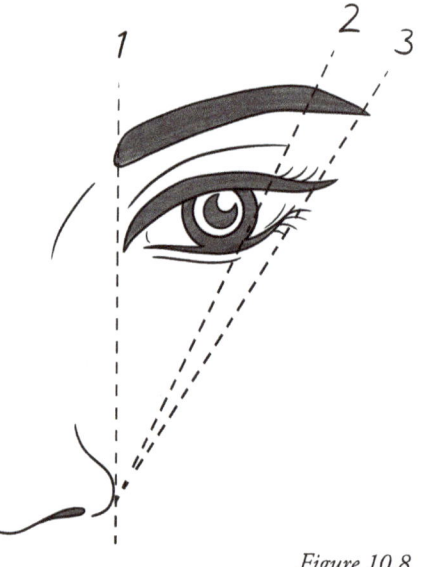

Figure 10.8

Enhancing Your Features: Face Shapes and Makeup

initially feel awkward, too dark, and bold. I can almost guarantee they are not. Check out Figure 10.7, which shows how much to fill in your eyebrows, and Figure 10.8 illustrates the ideal length of your brows.

- **Lips.** Do you love your lips? If so, play them up. You can use a lip liner to enlarge or decrease their size and shape (Figure 10.9). Be sure to fill in the entire lip so you do not risk that awful ring around your lips. Also, be sure your lip color accentuates your complexion and the clothes you wear. Consider changing the depth of color depending on the season and have a few lipstick shades to coordinate your lip color with your day's outfit.

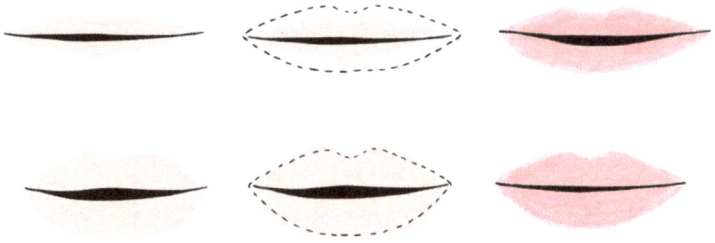

Figure 10.9

You can invest in makeup and know it will last. The ingredients are more important than the brand. As mentioned above, look for large makeup manufacturers for the best value. L'Oréal generates tens of billions annually with many brands under its umbrella, including Maybelline, Lancôme, NYX Professional Makeup, Urban Decay, and many more.[2] Estée Lauder owns several prestigious beauty brands, such as Estée Lauder, MAC Cosmetics, Clinique, Bobbi Brown, and Too Faced.[3] For a more budget-conscious option, Procter & Gamble is a multinational consumer goods company that owns brands like CoverGirl, Olay, and Max Factor.[4] There are many great brands to choose from.

BEARDS

Typically, men don't change the appearance of their faces with makeup; instead, they can alter their appearance dramatically due to their natural abundance of facial hair. Specific types of beards and mustaches come in and out of vogue. The first thing to ask yourself is what type appeals to you. Do you want a full beard or something that more resembles a five o'clock shadow? There are many apps to help you visualize yourself in a beard. Start by deciding on a direction and then be open to experimenting with different looks.

Specific beards complement certain face shapes more than others. For example, a goatee or full beard can add length to a round face, while a shorter, close-shaven beard can accentuate the jawline on a square face. A beard can help balance out a prominent chin or a long face; conversely, it can help a wider face look narrower. A beard can also make your jawline look stronger and perfectly defined. The oval face is the most symmetrical; therefore, if you have this face shape, feel free to experiment with any and all beard styles. Look at Figure 10.10 for the twenty most common beards and decide if you want to try one.

Enhancing Your Features: Face Shapes and Makeup

Figure 10.10

OVERALL IMPRESSIONS

Before we close out the chapter on faces, I should mention your smile because it is essential to your appearance and impression on others. Being uncomfortable with your smile affects how you carry yourself and interact with the world. I have had clients who refuse to smile. They raise their hand to cover their mouth to hide broken, missing, or yellow teeth. This is worse than showing your teeth needing repair; it makes you appear self-conscious and lacking in confidence. There are so many dental options today. Although it can be expensive, if you live with shame regarding your teeth, consider investing in yourself. Ask your dentist what solutions or referrals they have. Make this your priority.

Your face is an important canvas for personal expression. Understanding its shape can help you make informed decisions about your style. By choosing flattering necklines, learning makeup techniques, and for the men, considering beard styles, you can enhance your features and present your best self to the world.

Chapter 11

HAIR HARMONY: FINDING YOUR IDEAL STYLE AND STYLIST

I think the most important thing a woman can have next to her talent, of course, is her hairstylist.

—Joan Crawford

There are hundreds of different hairstyles for both men and women. Many of us will constantly change our style, while others pick one and stay with it for years. Hairstyles come in and out of fashion. If you haven't changed your cut and color in years, consider whether it still flatters you, communicates your brand, and shows that you are current and with the times. Just as with your wardrobe, annually reviewing your hairstyle is worthwhile. If you trust your hairstylist, ask them about the current trends and whether they think you need to consider a change.

Search online for the top cuts for women or men in your age range this year. You can add your adjectives to the search: creative, bold, edgy, sophisticated, modern, and so on. Also, consider your physical appearance, specifically your face shape, the type of hair you have (thick, thin, curly, straight, etc.), and whether you want the length to be long, medium, or short.

If you aren't 100% sure you have the best stylist, finding someone you can trust and with whom you are simpatico is a crucial step. When changing your current hairstyle, especially if it is a significant change, I recommend you find a master stylist. They will be the most expensive and experienced individuals in the salon. This is still my recommendation, even if you are on a budget. If you want to save money, look for someone who can easily follow the new style after you have a cut and color you love. It is much easier to maintain a style than it is to create a new one. Like any other professionals, some are more talented, reliable, and skilled than others. We trust our stylists to hone their craft and make us look stunning. Thankfully, a bad cut and color can be fixed, but usually at considerable cost. Do your due diligence in advance. Here are the steps I recommend:

- Pay attention to other people's hairstyles. If you see someone with a cut you admire and think would look good on you, approach them. Compliment them, and if they seem warm, ask who cuts their hair.
- Ask local friends, colleagues, and extended family—people you trust—if they have a hairstylist they would recommend.
- Post a question on social media or other online groups you frequent to ask for referrals.
- Research salons and stylists online. Read reviews and look for examples of the work of the individual stylists you might be considering.
- Not all master stylists are equal. Some specialize in certain hair types, textures, styles, and specific clientele. Make sure the stylist you pick is a match for your needs.
- Be sure to schedule a consultation before committing.
- Trust your gut. Did you enjoy the vibe of the salon? Were you able to communicate well? Did their ideas resonate with you? Did they have the skills and the commitment to ensure you are happy with the result? I once had a stylist whom I was delighted with, but she was so busy that when I had to reschedule, she couldn't fit me in for another month. I was forced to find someone else who was more available and flexible.

Hair Harmony: Finding Your Ideal Style and Stylist

The bottom line is that choosing the right stylist is essential. You will learn to trust them to make you look good, and it could be a long-term relationship. It's worth the extra time to make a good decision. When you find a new stylist or are ready for a consultation:

- Show up at your best. It's easy to skip doing your hair and makeup or to dress down for a hair appointment. I recommend against it, at least for your initial meeting. Remember the stats on first impressions? Seven seconds or less. Your new stylist will judge you based on your appearance and make recommendations based on what they see. Why not show up at your best?
- Tell them who you are. To be safe, don't leave their assumptions about you to guesswork. Tell them your adjectives, what you do for a living, and how you want the world to see you personally and professionally.
- Tell them about your lifestyle. Are you willing to put time into your hair every morning? Do you exercise or do sports and need to get your hair out of your face? Are you busy or low maintenance and know you won't make the time for blow drying, curling, or applying extra products? Be sure your stylist understands precisely how much time you will put into your new style so they can give you a cut that fits your lifestyle. We have all had the experience of loving the look when we leave the salon and then being unable to replicate it on our own. I recently had this happen with a new style, so I went back in, and my very accommodating stylist taught me how to blow dry my latest cut and the products I needed, which made all the difference.
- Consider your budget and how frequently you can visit the salon. Are you willing to go every five or six weeks, or do you prefer once a quarter? Find a style that will support you until your next visit, and understand how often that will be. Short hairstyles mean less time daily and more frequent visits to the

salon. A great color to cover your gray might leave you feeling young and vibrant, but you will need to get your roots covered more often. Maintaining your great look is essential, so don't overcommit.

- Consider your ideal style. Do you have a vision for your perfect hairstyle? How happy are you with your current style? How much latitude are you willing to give the stylist? Decide this in advance, and if you want to direct them to a style you have in mind, plan ahead and bring pictures to help them understand your vision.
- Evaluate your emotional willingness for change. The importance of this can't be overstated. If you are considering a change, make sure you are emotionally ready. A talented and trusted professional can advise you on what they believe will best show off your appearance and personality, but you should only do it if you're ready. Otherwise, you run the risk of hating your hair even if others love it.

I have clients with whom I've made suggestions for which they weren't ready. There are lots of reasons we stay stuck. Too many of my female clients still hear criticisms from their mothers in their heads and have limiting beliefs about what looks good on them. Others have a romantic partner who likes their hair a certain way, leaving them reluctant to make a change. Yes, hair will grow back, but it takes time. It's not like a new outfit that you can return. So to avoid feeling you made a mistake, make sure you are ready for a change.

Consider my client Mary Ellen whose willingness to listen to advice and make a change impressed me. She was content with her hair, but I knew she could do better. She is a strong, assertive, successful businesswoman and a jazz performer. In a workshop, I told her, when she felt ready, to do these things:

Hair Harmony: Finding Your Ideal Style and Stylist

1. Bring the length of her hair closer to her shoulders.
2. Part it on the other side—our faces are not symmetrical, and we all have one eye more prominent than the other. A side part should show off your larger, most lifted eye. Mary Ellen was showcasing her lower, less alert eye. My suggestion fixed that.
3. Change the color to vibrant red—the warm red hair color gave her beautiful contrast, allowing her to wear brighter colors in the boardroom and on stage. Plus, it made her blue eyes pop!
4. Add soft bangs and layers to offset the size of her forehead and bring attention to her eyes.

Mary Ellen already had a hair appointment for the next day. She did everything I suggested. Check out the results in Figure 11.0.

Before

After

Figure 11.0

Not everyone is ready to act immediately and risk such a dramatic change as Mary Ellen was at that moment. I have clients who have contacted me two years after such a recommendation to tell me they finally did it. They were happy they waited because they weren't emotionally ready and were now ecstatic with the change.

YOUR ULTIMATE STYLE BLUEPRINT

Mary Ellen's total transformation didn't occur overnight. Take a look at Figure 11.1 to see what I mean. She had more to change than just her hairstyle. She was brilliant but struggled with self-esteem and being heard in a male-dominated workplace. Unfortunately, this is not uncommon among my female clients. She often tried to hide her weight in loose-fitting, lifeless clothes, thinking they didn't matter and not wanting to spend time dressing a body she didn't love. But she knew she needed a change; she had hit the glass ceiling and was ready to invest in herself. After the new hairstyle, we worked on the rest: makeup, clothes, and accessories. Through this process, she gained a new sense of confidence and power. The men in her workplace noticed! She continues to move up the organizational chart. She is now one of the most respected members of her company's leadership team, overseeing international sales, a large team of men and women. Her new sense of style also boosted her confidence to rock the stage in her lifetime passion as a jazz singer. It all started with a rapid decision to change her hairstyle.

Let's assume you know you're ready and have found a stylist you want to work with; now what? It's a collaborative process. When I have had bad haircuts or color I didn't like, it was always because the stylist did what they wanted without discussing it with me. This is why communication is so important. Doing homework, looking for styles you like, and bringing photos to your appointment are worth it. When I help my clients find the right style, I consider many factors, and you can do the same. First, consider your brand adjectives and if your existing style is a match. Also, ask yourself if your hairstyle is current. It doesn't have to be trendy (unless that is one of your adjectives), but it should not be dated. This could immediately diminish your credibility, especially if you're advancing in age or in a cutting-edge career. I tell my clients to consider the words "current" and "relevant." This applies to your whole look. We never want to appear like we are still in the previous decade.

Hair Harmony: Finding Your Ideal Style and Stylist

Before
After

Figure 11.1

FACE SHAPE

When deciding on a hairstyle, consider your face shape and what will be most flattering to your features. Refer back to Figures 10.0 and 10.1 in Chapter 10 to review various face shapes.

- **Oval face.** As I've mentioned, this face shape is the most symmetrical. Hair that is short, long, straight, curly—anything that appeals to you will likely look terrific.
- **Oblong or rectangular face.** Many with this face shape would like it to appear more oval, making it seem shorter and, in the case of the oblong, broader. The best way to do this is with bangs that will shorten the appearance of your face. Long hair will make your face appear longer because it naturally draws the viewer's eye downward, so women with long faces are best in shorter hairstyles. To widen the appearance of your face, women can consider layers, especially around the cheekbones and chin, as well as wavy or curly hair.

If you are a man with this face shape, you should avoid hairstyles with volume on top since that will further elongate your face. Also, if you have a thin face, be careful not to have hair that is especially short on the sides, as that will make it appear even thinner. Textured haircuts with medium length on top and the sides are the best bet. A side part also works well.

- **Round or square face.** Many individuals with these face shapes aim to lengthen and thin their faces with their hairstyle. This is best accomplished by showing more of your face and avoiding bangs, potentially adding to the length with volume on top. Women may want to consider long layers starting from the jawline, which will help to lengthen the face. They may want to avoid cuts that end at their chin and instead look for ways to soften the appearance of the sharper lines.

    Men with a square face shape may be delighted to show off their angular edges. Men will likely do best to choose styles with short, tight sides, because any bulk on the sides will add to the width.

- **Heart- or diamond-shaped face.** People with these face shapes likely want to fill in around the chin. Bangs are an excellent choice for diamond face shapes. Women with these shapes often opt for long layers. Men with the diamond face shape should ideally avoid a haircut with short sides because it may accentuate the narrowness of the forehead. Since there isn't much a guy can do to fill in the narrow chin with his hairstyle, beards are often recommended for these face shapes.

Remember, all face shapes are beautiful. I have a client with a lovely heart-shaped face and a proportionately large forehead. When questioned, she said she loves her forehead and thinks it's sexy. There are no right or wrong answers when choosing any of this. It's up to you to decide what makes you feel handsome or beautiful. Please don't let me or anyone else impact what you see in the mirror.

HAIR TYPE

If you're considering a new hairstyle, it's also important to keep in mind the type of hair you have. Hair comes in many forms: straight, curly, thick, thin, coarse. You may love a style you find online, on a friend, or on a celebrity, but to know whether that style will look similar on you, you must understand how your hair grows and its natural composition. Your master stylist will realize this, and it will impact their recommendations. This might be the single biggest disconnect between client and stylist. We may want a style that isn't achievable based on the hair we have.

There are three hair categories:

- **The natural shape of your hair: straight, wavy, or curly.**
  If you don't fight what your hair does naturally, having a low-maintenance style that looks amazing on you is much easier. It is possible to have wavy or curly hair that is naturally straight, but it will take time both in the salon and at home. The same is true when you prefer straight hair to naturally curly locks.
- **The texture of each strand of hair: fine, medium, or coarse.**
  If you have fine hair, it is very soft with thin individual strands. Fine hair tends to be "flyaway" and hard to curl. It can take well to chemicals but gets damaged easily, especially if overly processed. If your hair has a medium texture (also called normal texture—the most common hair texture), it is the most manageable. This category takes perms and curls well. Finally, you have coarse hair if your hair strands are thick and wiry. As we age, normal hair can turn coarse because gray

hair is naturally wiry and coarse. The best aspect of this hair texture is that it is strong and won't damage easily. However, this hair type requires more processing time and doesn't take well to chemical treatments.
- **The amount of hair: thin or thick.** The simplest way to determine this is with the ponytail test. If you have enough hair, grab a scrunchie or rubber band, sweep your hair into a ponytail, and count the number of times the band wraps around your hair: more than three times means thin hair, two to three times means medium hair, and one time means thick hair. If it's not long enough for a ponytail, ask your hairstylist what type of hair you have and how it will impact your options.

You should also discuss the health of your hair and tips for keeping it healthy. Hair can become unhealthy due to illness, medications, exposure to harsh climates, or chemicals. This is important. You can do much more with your hair and it will look its best when it's healthy.

HAIR COLOR

You may also consider changing your hair color; this can dramatically affect your overall look at any age, especially as your hair grays. It is certainly okay to gray. Some men and women look fabulous in white or gray hair. Others, not so much. Consider your specific shade of gray and whether it complements your skin tone.

We previously discussed contrast levels and color harmony. Both factors are at play in determining your best hair color. Make sure a change of color, highlights, or color accents blend with your natural complexion. One thing to understand is that added color grabs your natural hair color. For example, if you are blonde with some underlying red and decide to add red to your hair, your hair will easily grab that added color.

Hair Harmony: Finding Your Ideal Style and Stylist

It will also be more likely to look natural and cohesive with your overall complexion than if you add a color that is not natural to you.

For years now, it's been popular for those looking for a bold, edgy, or creative look to add a few purple, pink, or blue strands to their hair. This is fun but rarely flattering. Usually, these are not hues that naturally blend with one's skin tone. It is a statement, but it often detracts from your beauty. Of course, this is okay; just consider the outcome. In this case, you would choose the statement that the edgy color and style are sending, compared to your most attractive appearance. Again, I recommend finding a talented master stylist and colorist who can advise you based on knowledge and experience.

It's fascinating how much goes into the chemistry of hair color. We each have body chemistry, and you'd be surprised by how that dynamic is at play when applying color to your hair. Your health, stress level, hormones, and even the medicine you take can affect how shades of color mix with your own hair color and your natural chemistry. For this reason, it is an excellent idea to share anything with your stylist that may impact the results of adding color to your hair, especially if you have previously experienced unexpected results.

Having a hairstyle that fits your personality, lifestyle, and features is one of the easiest things you can do to improve your appearance and confidence. It's with you everywhere you go. A new cut and color will provide you with immediate results. If you think you're ready for a change, go for it. Work with your current stylist or find someone new. This you can do today!

Chapter 12

COMPLETE YOUR LOOK: THE ART OF ACCESSORIZING

Accessories are like the finishing strokes of a painter's brush.
They highlight, define, and complete the masterpiece.

—Luly Yang

Accessorizing is the answer if you want to look polished and put together. For many women, this is the most challenging aspect of dressing; for men, it's often overlooked. How much or how little to accessorize is subjective. Some like a minimal approach while others enjoy adorning with enthusiasm. Regardless, the goal should be consistent with everything we have covered so far: cohesively communicate your brand and showcase your best features. It doesn't have to be expensive; it can be done effectively on any budget. The key is to be intentional with your execution. Understanding which accessories are right for you is what we will cover in this chapter.

Accessories are the finishing touches that pull your look together and include jewelry, scarves, ties and pocket squares, belts, hats, eyewear, bags, shoes, and socks and hosiery. We've discussed the importance of pulling outfits together in ways that complement your brand and showcase your features. Accessories are no exception and are indeed where the magic happens. Some of my clients simplify their clothing choices with classic styles in solid colors and then let the accessories create interest. This works exceptionally well for those who want to create a capsule wardrobe (outlined in the following chapter), where you can easily mix and match pieces to make many looks.

DETAILS TO CONSIDER

When thinking about which accessories to purchase, I recommend you start by focusing on your brand and making sure your accessories speak to your adjectives, your values, and the message you wish to convey. Next, leverage the elements of art we have discussed in previous chapters. Specifically consider these art elements and concepts when you choose which accessories to purchase and wear:

- **Shape.** Repeat the patterns of your best features and potentially the shapes and patterns in clothing items.
- **Proportion.** Consider where you are short and long and how specific accessories elongate or diminish your natural appearance.
- **Color.** Choose accessories that blend with and accentuate your color palette. An exception can be a color you love that is not in your natural color palette; use that color in a pair of shoes or another accessory not near your face.
- **Texture.** Consider adding dimension to your outfits by using a variety of textures in your accessories.
- **Scale.** Match your natural scale unless you are specifically interested in adding drama to an outfit (in which case you may want big and bold accessories).

For the most polished look, be consistent with the accessories you choose. They can tell a similar story by matching the same level of detail or artisanship. If, for example, you choose a piece of jewelry handmade by an artist from brushed metal, wood, or stone, then for your most cohesive look,

Complete Your Look: The Art of Accessorizing

all the other accessories you wear should be equally rough and natural. Items made from metal or other rigid materials, wood, woven fabrics, or leather (real, faux, or vegan) complement one another beautifully. On the other hand, fine jewelry that is sophisticated and exquisitely designed, gold, platinum, diamonds, and other gemstones work best together, complemented with a delicate silk scarf, refined designer eyewear, and couture shoes.

If you are like most of my clients, learning to accessorize well will take time. Start by asking yourself some basic questions:

- Do you want to wear just a few pieces of high-end jewelry daily, or do you prefer a wide array of jewelry?
- Do you have an extensive shoe collection (or aspire to acquire one) that allows you to change the appearance of outfits simply by changing your shoes, or are you more practical with your footwear?
- What other finishing touches do you possess: scarves, ties, hats, belts, bags, eyewear?
- Do you like to have many choices and therefore a lower-cost option is best, or are you all about designer things and therefore less is best for you?

Also, consider how many accessories you want to wear at one time—some love to accessorize with hats, scarves, and multiple pieces of jewelry, and others don't. There is no right or wrong approach. However, you may appear understated with no accessories and a bit overdone with too many. I like to consider it an art form with many variables. Different outfits, people, and occasions warrant different approaches. I have a personal formula for jewelry, and you might find your own. I either wear a statement necklace or statement earrings, but never both or neither. I usually wear a fashion cocktail ring on my right hand and a bracelet or watch on my left hand. I also almost always have my nails manicured, which I consider an additional finishing touch. This formula intuitively suits me and the style

I wish to convey. I bet you will find yours over time. Let's consider all the accessories:

JEWELRY

Jewelry is not just for women; it's a great enhancement to a man's wardrobe, and you are no longer limited to just a wedding band. Necklaces, bracelets, earrings (to a lesser degree), and rings are all worn by the modern man. When it comes to jewelry, you can choose a few high-quality, classic designer pieces to wear daily; lots of interesting, handmade items; or even colorful mass-produced items. I have a combination of all the above. What jewelry to wear and when is nuanced and challenging since there are so many options from which to choose. Of course, you should consider your brand, color palette, and scale. Let's start with necklaces. The most common options are shown in Figure 12.0.

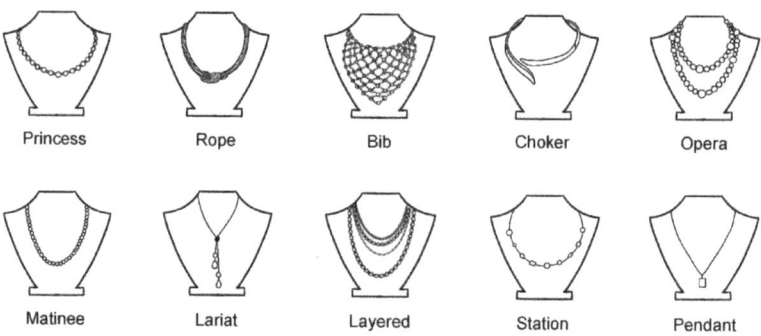

Figure 12.0

Determining which to incorporate into your wardrobe will depend heavily on your preference, personality, and lifestyle. Although most of these necklaces are worn more by women than by men, men do commonly wear necklaces. Typically, they only own a few, and they are on the understated side. The pendant seen in Figure 12.0 is an example of

Complete Your Look: The Art of Accessorizing

a man's necklace. Men sometimes prefer a simple chain, dog tags, or a religious symbol.

Earrings are also worn by both men and women, again more commonly by women and in more styles. Check out Figure 12.1 for the most common earring types.

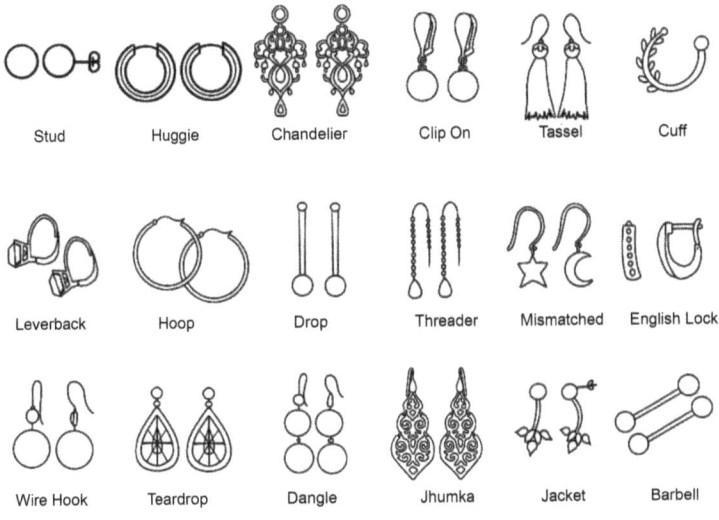

Figure 12.1

As you decide the best necklaces and earrings for you, you may wish to consider your face shape. If you have an oval face, you have the most flexibility because your face is very symmetrical; from necklaces to earrings, you can wear what you like. Using shapes that bring attention to your best features, like circles for your eyes or mimicking the shape of your face, will work especially well.

Some women with oval faces like sets like the one shown in Figure 12.2, but many prefer to mix and match for more interest.

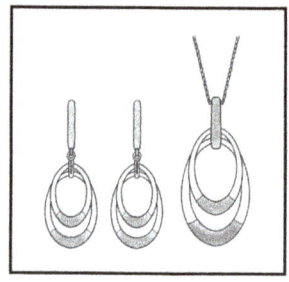

Oval Face Type

Figure 12.2

For a round or square face, try long, dangling earrings and necklaces to help elongate your face (Figure 12.3).

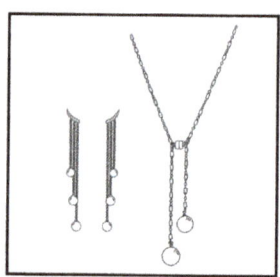

Round and Square Face Type

Figure 12.3

Complete Your Look: The Art of Accessorizing

For a heart- or diamond-shaped face, earrings wider at the bottom, such as chandeliers or teardrops, will balance out your narrower chin. You might also like shorter necklaces, like a choker or collar style (Figure 12.4).

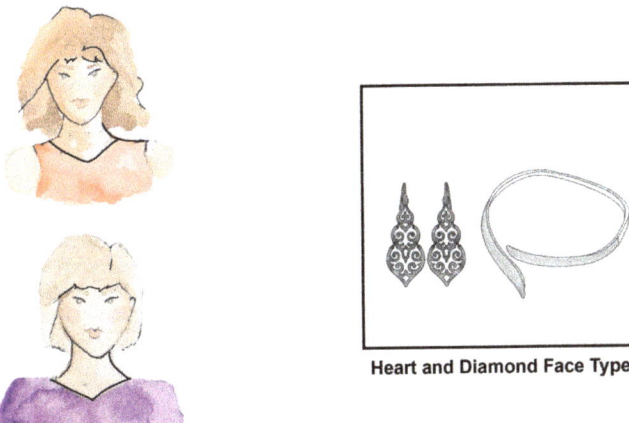

Heart and Diamond Face Type

Figure 12.4

An oblong face looks most balanced with jewelry that widens your face, such as stud earrings with large gemstones, hoops, and chandelier styles. Necklaces with bold and chunky designs, layered necklaces, or mix-and-match styles draw attention to the neck and chest area, creating width and balance (Figure 12.5).

 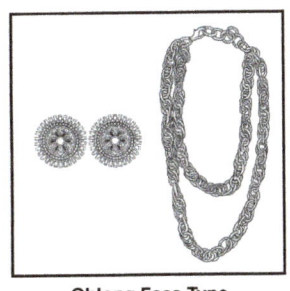

Oblong Face Type

Figure 12.5

YOUR ULTIMATE STYLE BLUEPRINT

Do you feel your neck is too long or too short? The average neck length is four inches. It will likely be a bit longer if you are tall with a long head, or shorter if you are petite. In some cultures, people find a long neck feminine and beautiful, whereas a shorter neck might be deemed more masculine. Take a look in the mirror and decide for yourself. If you have a long neck and want it to appear shorter, choose chokers and post earrings. If you have a short neck, do the opposite: opt for delicate and dainty necklaces, longer necklaces, and dangling earrings to create vertical lines.

Bracelets are another common jewelry item worn by both men and women. As with the other items, your color palette, scale, personality, lifestyle, and budget are the most significant factors in deciding what to wear. Check out Figure 12.6 for common bracelet styles.

Rings are another form of jewelry worn by most people. Promise and engagement rings, wedding bands, class rings, and rings with birthstones are commonly worn and don't require an explanation. These may be rings you wear every day. Look at Figure 12.7 for other typical options.

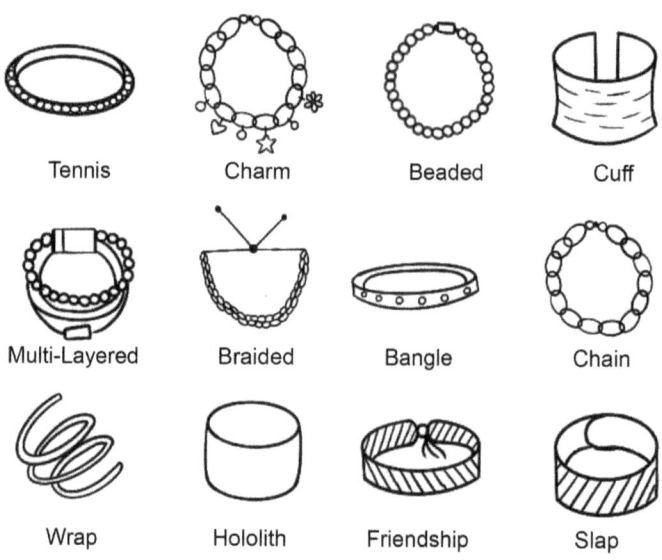

Figure 12.6

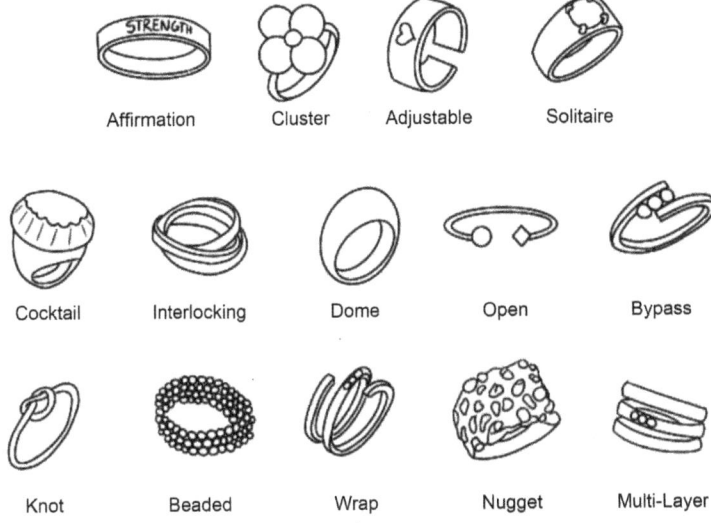

Figure 12.7

Many other types of jewelry are also commonly worn, such as:

- Brooches and pins can feel formal or old-fashioned but also come in fun and modern designs.
- Anklets are a popular accessory in warmer climates and seasons, worn by both men and women, especially young people.
- Hair jewelry, including hairpins, clips, bands, tiaras, and headbands, can be adorned with jewels, pearls, and other decorative elements.
- Nose rings and studs have become popular with younger generations of men and women.
- Toe rings, like anklets, are often seen in warmer climates and cultures and can be made of metal, elastic, or other materials.
- Watches, beyond their practical use, can be a fashion statement and a symbol of style and status.
- Cufflinks are used primarily by men for shirts with French cuffs and are functional and decorative.

YOUR ULTIMATE STYLE BLUEPRINT

- Tie clips and tie bars, worn chiefly by men, are both decorative and functional to keep a tie in place while adding a touch of style.

As you can see, there are many options when it comes to jewelry, all of which make a statement about who you are and help create a polished look. If you want to take your style to the next level, start to add well-selected pieces of jewelry to your wardrobe. But don't stop there. There are other accessories to consider.

SCARVES

Scarves can be worn by both men and women. They can make a statement by adding interest and color to both casual and professional looks. Look at Figure 12.8 for scarf ideas for men.

Figure 12.8

Complete Your Look: The Art of Accessorizing

Women wear scarves for many reasons and in many ways. They can be a colorful substitute for a necklace, worn for warmth, an accessory to a handbag, and more. Like necklaces, they are best worn differently based on your face shape. For example, if you have a round face, a long scarf draped around your neck will elongate your silhouette. If you have a square face, you might prefer a soft, flowing scarf that will soften the angles of your face. If you have an oblong face, a scarf that is wider than it is long could help balance your features. A scarf can fill the chin area for diamond- and heart-shaped faces. Look at Figure 12.9 for some ways women can add a scarf to their look.

Figure 12.9

TIES

Ties can be worn by both men and women but are more common for men. As discussed in previous chapters, the first thing to consider is the size and color, relating back to your scale and color palette. If you are a large and tall guy, most definitely wear a wide tie; a thin guy should wear a thin tie; and an average man—you guessed it—should wear a tie that is neither wide nor thin. Look at Figure 12.10 for an example of how different-sized ties work best with an individual's scale. Men now wear suits and ties less often than in the past, and when worn, you have more liberty to wear exciting and creative colors and patterns. If it fits your brand and personal style, go for it, get creative, and have fun with it. And remember to play around with a pocket square for added panache.

Figure 12.10

BELTS

Belts offer more latitude in color and size than many other accessories because they are not worn near your face. However, both men and women should consider the scale of their bodies and match the width of their belts and belt buckles to their physique. For women, consider your proportions. Go back to Chapter 7 and reflect on whether you are long- or short-waisted, tall or petite. Where you wear a belt—how low or high it is around your waist and hips—can emphasize or diminish your body proportions in a positive or negative light. Also, review your shape. If you are a woman with an hourglass or triangle-shaped figure, elastic waist belts will be incredibly flattering and show off your thin waist. One rule

Complete Your Look: The Art of Accessorizing

everyone should follow is that if you have belt loops that show, always wear a belt.

Take a look at Figure 12.11 to help you decide which types of belts will most flatter your shape and fit with your wardrobe.

Men don't have much of a selection when it comes to belts. One easy choice is to opt for belts that match your shoes. This is not a hard rule but a common practice and a simple place to start. If you have camel, navy, and black shoes, start with belts in these colors. The primary factors are the style, shape, size of the buckle, and material used for the belt. The buckle is ideally best if it matches your color palette: silver or brushed chrome for cool-complected individuals and gold for warm-toned people. The belt material can range from canvas to alligator. Choose what you like based on your brand and lifestyle. Figure 12.12 gives an idea of the types of belts and buckles men may want to consider.

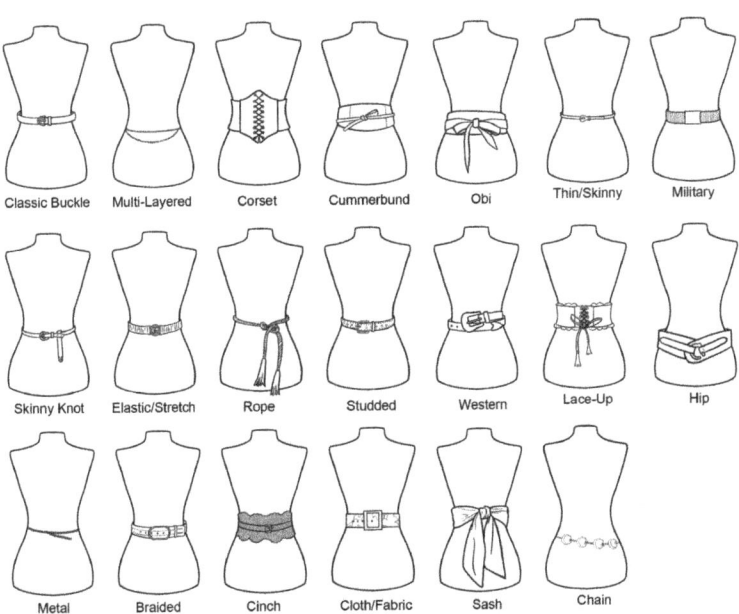

Figure 12.11

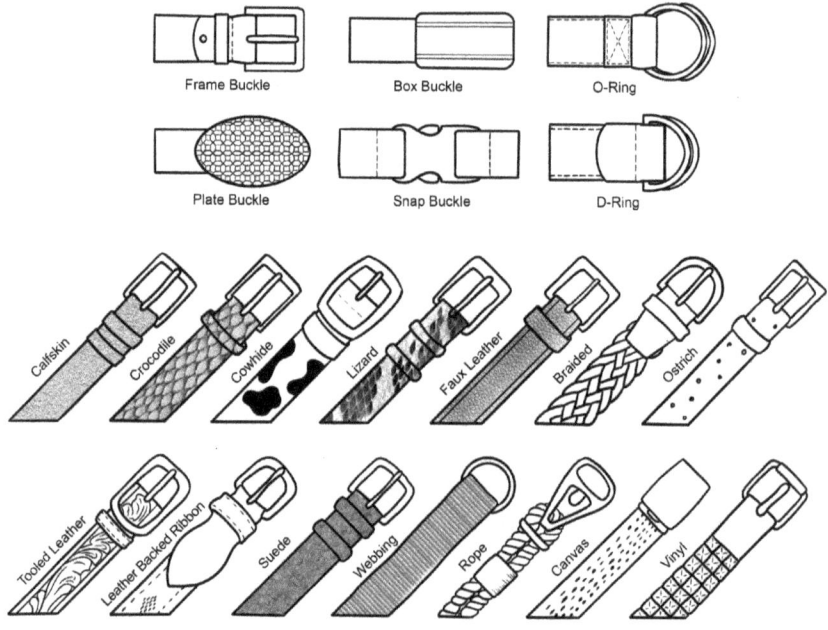

Figure 12.12

EYEWEAR

Eyewear can dramatically impact your appearance. Whether you wear readers, shades, or glasses all day to see, consider investing in a variety of styles. This used to be difficult for anyone on a budget because the cost of prescription eyewear was a more significant factor than it is today. Most of us had to settle for one essential pair that would go with everything, leaving them nondescript and uninteresting. Thankfully, times have changed. Now, companies like Warby Parker have brought the cost of eyewear to the point where function, fashion, and affordability are all attainable. If you have the money to spend, many eyewear boutiques sell exquisite designer frames. No matter your budget, you can own a variety of specs, an accessory worth the investment. Look at Figure 12.13 for a glossary of eyewear's most common styles and shapes.

Complete Your Look: The Art of Accessorizing

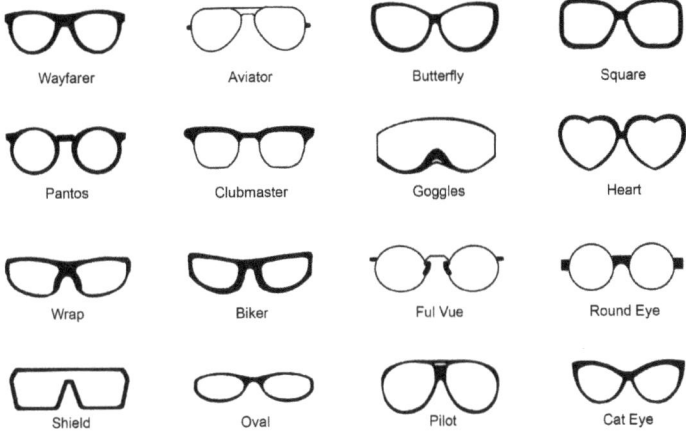

Figure 12.13

Choosing the proper eyewear can be confusing, so I created an acronym to help my clients: GETSPECS. Here's what it means:

- **G**o up. This is important for those of us of a certain age. If you are fighting a gravitational pull downward, use your eyewear to create lift, especially in the outer upper edges. Some styles have this naturally; for others, you can look for embellishments in the frames to accomplish this goal (Figure 12.14).

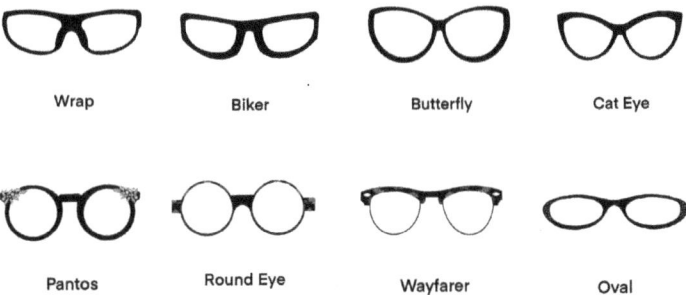

Figure 12.14

- **Equal.** The distance from your eyes to the outer and inner edges of the lens should be equal. Your PD (pupil distance) is an important measurement. Not only is this critical technically, but it also looks best when your eyes are centered in the lens. To find out whether you have wide or narrow eyes, measure your eye width. Could you place a third eye over the bridge of your nose? If so, your eyes are neither wide nor narrow. If you have wider eyes, you should buy wider frames. If your eyes are narrow, then narrow frames are better for you. Many stores have their inventory laid out in this manner to help you choose correctly.
- **Temple.** The glasses' temples should not touch your face or have a large gap between the temple and your face. More than a finger's width between the temple and your face indicates the frames are too broad.
- **Shape.** The shape of the frames should support your face shape. If you have a square face, your glasses should be angular; if you have a round face, round glasses will be flattering, and so on (Figure 12.15).
- **Personal Brand.** Your glasses can tell a definite story. I've mentioned this before: consider your brand. Do you want something edgy, sophisticated, modern, or feminine?
- **Eyebrows.** Make sure your frames mimic your eyebrow's shape or cover them altogether. But don't fight the shape. This is one thing most often overlooked. Take a look at the difference in Figure 12.16.

Complete Your Look: The Art of Accessorizing

Figure 12.15

Figure 12.16

- **Color.** You know your colors. Make sure your eyewear complements your complexion.
- **Scale.** Keep your scale in mind. If you are petite, avoid overwhelming your face with large-scale glasses. If you are more significant, consider statement glasses that are right for your stature. I know large-scale glasses are currently trending. It's okay to make a fashion statement if you love them, but if you are petite, they may not be the most flattering.

HATS

Hats are fun and attention-grabbing—an underrated accessory that can add interest to your style. My husband wears a hat almost daily; it has become part of his persona. He is a man of a certain age, and he didn't wear hats as a young man, although he certainly could have. He somehow feels it's an older gentleman's thing. He is commonly complemented on his hats and how they add to his personal style. See Figure 12.17 for a glossary of hats to consider.

Find time to go to a hat store, try different types, snap pics, and decide what you like. Start with one and go from there. Here are some guidelines to consider when purchasing a hat:

- Your hat should balance out your dimensions rather than exaggerate them: tall crowns and upturned brims are lengthening, while broad and down-turned brims make you appear shorter.
- A hat's brim should be no wider than the width of your shoulders.
- The larger your build, the more "hat" you can get away with.

You are likely noticing a theme. It's all about your shape and proportions, not to mention color, scale, and personal brand. Just start thinking in these terms about everything you wear!

Complete Your Look: The Art of Accessorizing

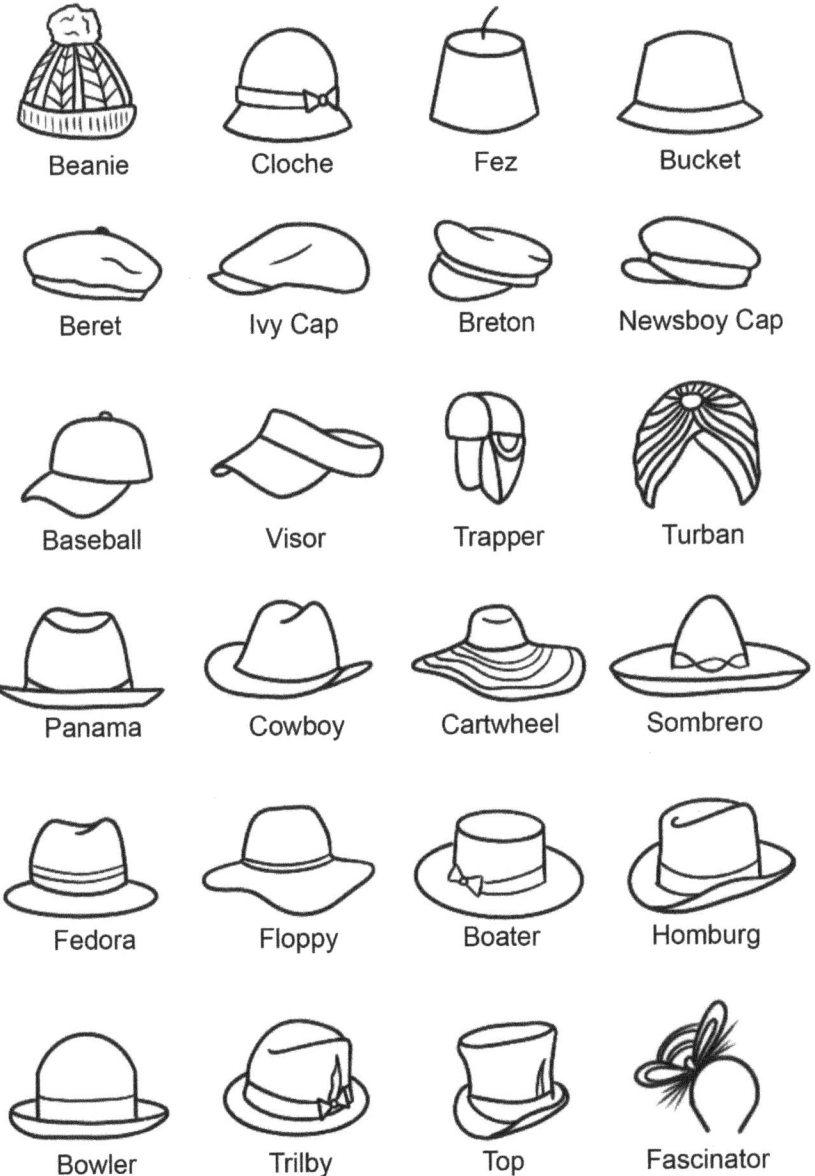

Figure 12.17

BAGS

Whether it's a purse, wallet, briefcase, or backpack, the bag you carry can add to or detract from your appearance. Of course, you will consider what supports your lifestyle. Consider whether the bag communicates quality, creativity, status, practicality, or sophistication. Do you want just one that works with all the other items in your wardrobe or many that you can use as a fun complement to your outfit of the day? When choosing bags, consider how they relate to your body shape and scale:

- If you have a larger frame, a bigger bag with structure will help balance out your silhouette.
- If you have straight lines and want to appear curvier, consider a slouchy bag, which can add curves to your look.
- If you are petite, an oversized bag can make you appear even smaller, so it's better to match your smaller scale.
- The most harmonious choice is to match the shape of your bag to the shape of your face.

See Figure 12.18 for a glossary of the various styles of bags.

I know women who have different bags for every outfit in their wardrobe and others who limit their bags to one or two, only changing them up for the season of the year. Decide what works for you and challenge yourself to slowly add bags to complement the many different occasions of your life.

Complete Your Look: The Art of Accessorizing

Figure 12.18

YOUR ULTIMATE STYLE BLUEPRINT

SHOES, SOCKS, AND HOSE

I love shoes. Many call them the foundation of your outfit. Indeed, they make a statement, whether good or bad. I have shoes that are stunning yet very hard to walk in, so I only put them on when I am sitting more than standing. But more and more, I look for shoes that are both comfortable and attractive. There are so many beautiful but comfortable shoes these days. You can find shoes of any height, from six-inch stilettos to block heels, and even flats are made with style.

I love the sneaker craze from the comfort era associated with the pandemic. I own five pairs of Chuck Taylors in various colors and patterns; a few are rebranded by top designers, like Dolce & Gabbana, Gucci, and Coach. But be mindful. A pair of sneakers or comfort shoes with a white rubber sole isn't a good match for formal affairs. Not long ago, a photo captured (then) Speaker of the House Kevin McCarthy, Senator Mitch McConnell, and Representative Hakeem Jeffries wearing a version of the sneaker shoe in the Oval Office. It was all over the papers and the news criticizing their disrespect of the occasion. It's an example of taking a style too far, but at least it was a bipartisan blunder.

Check out Figure 12.19 for a glossary of shoes for both men and women.

Here are my tips on buying the right shoes for you:

- Buy as many pairs as you can afford, but focus on quality over quantity.
- Keep them in tip-top shape. Worn-out shoes will complement no one's brand.
- Women, match the heel to your stature. Consider chunkier shoes if you have large ankles and calves; if you have thin legs and ankles, slim stilettos or kitten heels will look best.
- Be comfortable. Limping in uncomfortable shoes ruins the look.

Complete Your Look: The Art of Accessorizing

Figure 12.19

YOUR ULTIMATE STYLE BLUEPRINT

- If you want a polished look, match your toe box to the rest of your outfit or physical appearance: round face, round toe box; diamond- or heart-shaped face, pointy toe; and so on. If you want to look put together, take it one step further and match your neckline to your face shape and toe box—for example, a heart-shaped face, V-neck, and pointy toe. Check out Figure 12.20 to see what I mean.
- Ladies, as we covered previously, avoid ankle straps with dresses unless you have long legs or don't mind them looking shorter. If you want your legs to look longer, match the color of your leg. That is your pant leg, tights, or skin tone; remember, nude is not the same for all of us.

Socks and hosiery of all types can also be fun accessories. Depending on the look you want to project and your body proportions, try fun patterns or wear classic colors that match your skin, pants, or shoes.

Accessorizing can be fun. It is an art form. Get creative and think about which accessories you like. You don't have to have them all, but it's an easy way to add variety to your wardrobe, especially if you're on a budget.

Figure 12.20

Chapter 13

WARDROBE MASTERY: BUILDING A CLOSET FULL OF CLOTHES THAT INSPIRE YOU TO BE YOUR BEST

Any item in your wardrobe should satisfy one of two criteria: utility and joy.
—Stacy London

So far, everything you've learned has given you insight into why your appearance matters and how to create a brand, image, and style. In this chapter, we will pull it all together, showing you how to review the clothes and accessories you own, how to shop with intention, and how to build a style you love.

Every item you purchase matters. Having a wardrobe that shows you at your best and fosters self-confidence can be expensive. According to a study conducted by ClosetMaid, the average American woman has around 103 items of clothing in her wardrobe, excluding accessories.[1] Further data tells us the typical American spends between $40 to $60 on average on each item of nonluxury apparel. Therefore, the typical American woman has a wardrobe worth over $5,150 ($50 per item x 103 clothing items). From my experience, these numbers are low. This data includes low-end brands and previously owned clothing, so if you prefer higher-end luxury goods, your numbers will be much higher.

YOUR ULTIMATE STYLE BLUEPRINT

How big is your wardrobe and how much do you spend per item? It's worth knowing because here is another critical statistic from a ClosetMaid survey: "Most people only wear 20% of the items they own."[2] This means that, in our example, a typical individual has $4,120 of clutter hanging in their closet (again, I think this number is low). Regardless, our goal should be to limit the clothes we own to those we love and wear—the 20%. I have clients who own one hundred pairs of shoes and many others who prefer a much more limited selection of items from which to choose their look of the day. Either way, the objective of the Ultimate Style Blueprint is to understand your personal brand, use art principles to dress to showcase your features, and love the clothes you own and wear all of them.

I recommend you start with a complete closet analysis. When I have a new client, this is our next step after I have helped them discover their Ultimate Style Blueprint: They look at the clothes they own to decide if they are a match. Culling your wardrobe can be time-consuming and frustrating. You will likely find a closet full of clothes that don't give you joy, don't communicate your brand, or don't meet your Ultimate Style Blueprint and garments you find to be tired, worn, and dated. I promise this process and the ensuing results are worth the time. Just like spring cleaning, the feeling of purging and streamlining is empowering. Start by asking yourself the following questions:

- What does each item I own communicate? Is that the message I want to convey about myself?
- Is it a good color for me?
- Are the shape, scale, and proportions right for my body?
- What about the neckline?
- How is the fit?
- Most importantly, how do I feel when I put on each item?

Be selective. You deserve to feel amazing every day in the clothes you wear!

Keep in mind that we can feel an emotional attachment with our things, which can make it hard to let them go. We hold on to garments because we are convinced that one day we will need them or because they represent moments in time we cherish, we feel guilty, or we don't want to be wasteful. I tell my clients that having unused clothing in their closets could be considered wasteful—many people genuinely need and could benefit from your unwanted things. Plus, they are taking space away from a replacement item that could make you feel confident and empowered, that could make you feel like a million bucks.

After the first closet analysis I recommend culling your clothes at least once a year. I do it twice annually. I live in greater Washington, DC, where there are distinct seasons. I review my clothes in April or May and October to prepare for warmer or cooler weather. For example, I move all my cold weather clothes into bins in the spring. But first I assess each item and ask myself the following:

- Did I wear it, and did it provide me joy and confidence?
- Is it still in good shape, or is it worn, torn, or damaged?
- Is the item a classic design and still fashionable, or is it a bit dated?
- Does it fit well, or has it stretched or shrunk in size?
- Has my body shifted so it is no longer flattering? If so, is my shift temporary or permanent?
- Do I love the item but have nothing to wear with it? We refer to these items as orphans.

Based on the answers to these questions, I decide whether to keep items for the following year, move them into containers marked "aspirational," get them altered, or sell, donate, or trash them, and shop for matches for the orphans. I believe in limiting the clothes hanging in my closet to those that I will wear now. If they don't fit, are for a different season, or are merely sentimental, out of style, or worn out, then they are clutter. I include my shoes in this process. Are they worn, uncomfortable, unused, or seasonal? If so, I move them out of my view temporarily or permanently.

Clutter negatively impacts how we feel about the experience of getting dressed. Let's make your closet a place you love to be, a space that inspires you. If you have a walk-in closet, consider decorating it with lovely lighting, paint colors, fixtures, and furniture. Regardless, think of ways to organize it as clutter-free as possible. Start with quality matching hangers. Wood hangers are probably the best, but if you have limited space, I also like the thin velvet hangers.

It's also important to create a system that helps you see what you wear and don't wear on an ongoing basis. You could start the year or season with all your hangers facing in one direction and turn them around as you wear each item. Another option is to tie a ribbon around the hanging rod in your closet and move clothes to the other side after you wear them. I buy those rings that separate and label sizes often seen in boutiques and department stores. When I wear something, I hang a ring on the hanger to indicate what has been worn. Whichever method you adopt, try to wear things you haven't, breaking the habit of wearing the same items and outfits repetitively. If you notice you aren't wearing certain pieces, ask yourself why. These are the typical reasons:

- You don't feel good or inspired by an item—it doesn't communicate who you are or match your Ultimate Style Blueprint.
- It doesn't fit correctly.
- It's dated or worn, and you don't feel good in it.
- You have nothing to wear with it; it's an orphan.

The most important task in building a wardrobe you love is to analyze the clothes you already own. This helps you be more mindful when you shop. That's why most often, with new clients, shopping comes last. Before we engage in this task, we create a list of items that we determine are missing. That way when we shop, we can do so with set objectives, instead of buying more random pieces that we aren't sure how they will be worn. When you are ready to shop, ask yourself these questions:

- What items are on my list—what do I need and what do I already own?
- Do I love to shop, and what stores and boutiques do I enjoy?
- Is shopping instead an arduous task, and if so should I shop online?
- How much do I want to spend?
- What type of wardrobe do I want to own?
- What is my lifestyle?
- What are my values?
- Do I have any cultural or religious dress requirements?
- Do I require specialty sizing?

These questions are explored in the remainder of this chapter.

First, consider your priorities—what are your most pressing needs and where is the best place to shop for those pieces? If you aren't sure, I recommend doing some initial online research to learn where you might find the items you seek. Ask yourself where you enjoy shopping. It's ideal to find a store or some boutiques that inspire you, where the shop's brand matches yours and the styles tend to fit you well. It's even more productive and pleasant when you find a store or shop where you can develop a relationship with a sales clerk.

Most of my clients "hate" to shop. They find it overwhelming and exhausting. If this is you, you definitely need a plan before you walk out the door. You might even prefer online shopping. I'm a fan of shopping online, but there are pros and cons. Access to inventory is a significant advantage. For example, when I shop in person at a department store or national chain, I am limited to that store's inventory. However, when I shop that store online, I gain access to their inventory at all of their locations nationwide. Additionally, their robust search engine allows me to parse the things I'm seeking: size, color, brand, price, style, and so on. I can also check reviews that can help me vet a particular item.

On the negative side, it's easier to make mistakes when shopping online. You can't touch and feel the quality of the fabric, and it can be challenging to predict how things will fit. The model shown in pictures is typically six feet tall and very thin. Since that doesn't match our silhouette for most of us, it takes experience and some imagination to see the difference in how each item will look on our shape and size.

With that said, as you apply your Ultimate Style Blueprint, it gets easier. The mistakes you might make won't be fatal if you are diligent about returns. When I shop online, I am strict with myself and my clients, insisting the items that arrive in the mail are treated with the same critical eye as if they were taken into a dressing room at the store. But in this case it's a better dressing room: a benefit to online shopping is trying on items in your home. You have better lighting, reliable mirrors, and proper undergarments at home. You have the bonus of being able to try on your new items with things you already own. For those who "hate" to shop, the convenience of online shopping has a tremendous net positive result.

You also want to consider your budget. Are you tight on funds, can you buy whatever you want whenever you want, or are you somewhere in between? It's important to consider all the things you need. If, after your closet analysis, you realize you need a whole new wardrobe, you may need to budget. This may direct your priorities and where to shop. I have a philosophy: never pay retail. I break this rule occasionally, like during an exotic vacation when I want to splurge on something unique or sentimental or for a special event. But most of the time, I buy off-season when things are on sale, at consignment shops, or at premium outlet stores.

Like cars, wardrobe items significantly lose value when they leave the showroom floor. Buying secondhand is especially value-packed. You can find many small shops in your area, and national and international online sites are now plentiful. As with everything else, you can return items that aren't as expected or don't fit you perfectly. Again, be discerning. If this approach doesn't appeal to you, if you like to buy new things in the heart of the season or at high-end specialty stores, that's fantastic. The choice and approach are very personal. Do what works for you and your household budget.

Also consider the type of wardrobe you want to own. There are two distinct options: a capsule wardrobe where you buy a variety of separates that you can mix and match, or specialty pieces that are fabulous enough to stand alone. Most of my clients choose a combination of these two approaches.

CAPSULE WARDROBE

Like a capsule in medicine, a capsule wardrobe is a concentrated dose of essential items that provide everything you need in one container. A typical capsule wardrobe might include thirty to forty pieces, including tops, bottoms, dresses, jackets, and outerwear. The idea is to focus on quality over quantity, investing in pieces that will last for years and stay in style. The variety of outfits you can create by utilizing this approach is incredible. Think about the results of mixing and matching five bottoms (skirts and pants) with ten tops. That's fifty different combinations. What if you add five jackets to those fifty outfits? That takes it to 250 unique looks. You could also have five dresses in addition to the five jackets, giving you twenty-five additional looks.

This formula doesn't consider accessories; adding shoes, scarves, and jewelry combinations can completely change the appearance of an outfit. This approach will allow you to streamline your closet with an expansive variety of looks by considering the most complementary colors, shapes, and proportions and finding items that work well together. Look at Figure 13.0 for a simplified illustration of a capsule wardrobe based on our scenario above, with just one pair of pants plus five tops and five jackets plus the option to wear no jacket: $1 \times 5 \times (5+1) = 30$. You can see how your wardrobe could exponentially grow using this system.

YOUR ULTIMATE STYLE BLUEPRINT

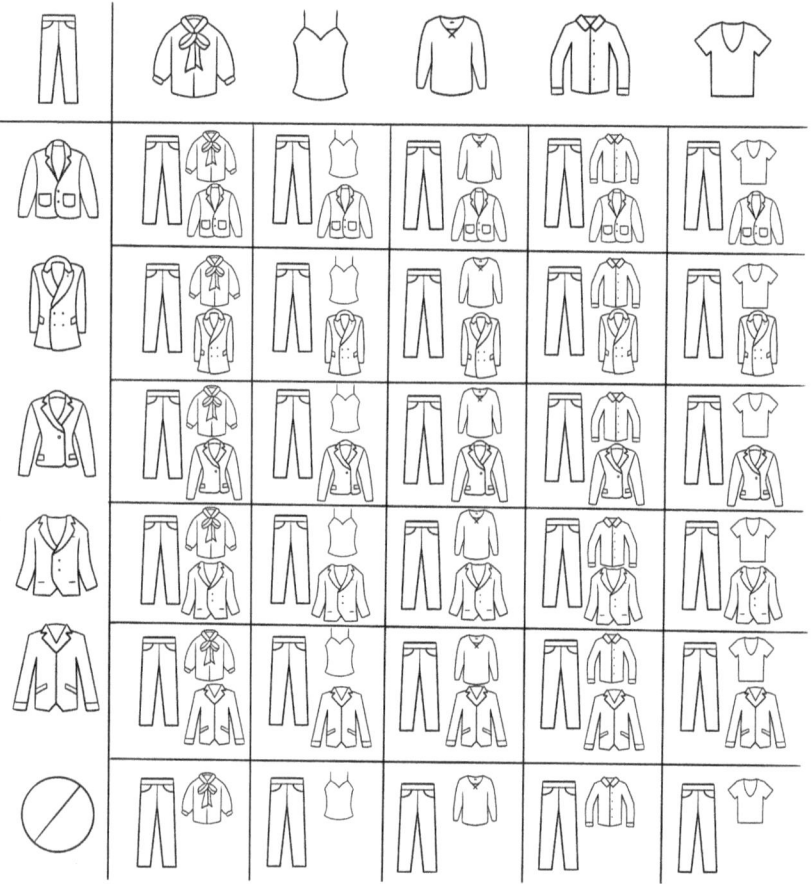

Figure 13.0

Steve Jobs and Elizabeth Holmes are famous for taking this concept to extremes. Jobs was known for his distinctive and minimalist fashion style. He wore the same outfit daily: a black turtleneck, blue jeans, and white sneakers. This may not be for all of us, but his fashion choices were in alignment with his brand. He believed that good design should be intuitive and easy to use, and his fashion choices reflected this belief. His iconic look has since become a part of his legacy, representing his unconventional approach to technology and fashion. Interestingly, Elizabeth Holmes deliberately followed suit, often wearing black turtlenecks with black slacks and a black blazer. This uniform is now considered by many as another way she presented a false sense of competence and authority.

I advocate for the capsule wardrobe, but not to those extremes. They are too much like uniforms and completely uninteresting. You can simplify while still bringing color, interest, individuality, and creativity into your wardrobe.

STORYTELLING OUTFITS

Another approach is using storytelling outfits, which include things like tuxedos, gowns, or other items that are unique and interesting enough to stand on their own. You might fall in love with an incredible design, a bright color, or a pattern, something worth the investment to wear only on occasion and only as it is without the need to pair it with other items. Storytelling outfits require a bigger budget because they require significantly increasing the size of your wardrobe.

Most clients prefer to start with a capsule wardrobe and add some one-of-a-kind (storytelling) outfits for special occasions. I often get asked how many pieces of clothing I recommend each person own. I don't have a direct answer because it's a very individual choice. It has a lot to do with preferences and lifestyle. For example, I have clients who refuse to wear dresses and skirts. They aren't fond of their legs, and nothing I say can change that. On the other hand, I have clients who prefer dresses to slacks. Some never wear jackets; they have a more casual lifestyle and select sweaters for cooler weather. So it depends on you. After you have completed your closet analysis and have pared down your clothes to the "keepers," assess what you have and what you need to generate as many combinations as possible. That will indicate the number of items you should pursue.

LIFESTYLE CHOICES

How do you live? What are your professional and personal wardrobe needs? Do you work in person or mostly remotely? Do you do presentations where you need to step it up? Do you need business casual attire as well as more formal wear? What do you wear after work and on the weekends? Do you go out? Do you vacation? Do you have kids and need clothes for activities with them? Do you exercise? Think about how you live and what clothes are required to support you. You will, of course, need to consider where you live, how varied the climate is, and how that affects your seasonal wardrobe. In this step, I recommend you list everything you do, from going to the gym to hanging out with your kids, dressing for church, date night, and more. If the list is different in warm weather months compared to cooler months, note that. Then consider whether you have enough clothing items for each occasion that leave you feeling your best, most attractive, and confident. This should arm you with the information you need to assess your current wardrobe needs.

Also, ask yourself if you want to factor in your values. Does that sound like a strange question when thinking about building a wardrobe? You might be surprised to learn the fashion industry significantly impacts the environment and is responsible for 10% of global carbon emissions. That is more than the emissions from all international flights and maritime shipping combined. Beyond these issues, workers in the fashion industry are often subject to long hours, low wages, and unsafe working conditions. Fashion production is one of the most significant users of forced labor, with an estimated sixteen million people working in forced labor conditions. I don't want you to feel guilty about buying clothes. We need clothes. I love clothes—they help us express who we are. It gives us pleasure to shop and dress—everything we have discussed so far in this book. But if you want to be mindful about your wardrobe and the associated societal costs, these are facts you should know, and there are ways to work around them.

SUSTAINABILITY

Conscious clothing, a growing movement, is focused on sustainable and ethical fashion practices and aims to reduce the impact of fashion on the environment, animals, and people. This can include using eco-friendly materials such as organic cotton, recycled polyester, or innovative fabrics from seaweed, bamboo, or mushroom leather. It can also involve fair labor practices and ensuring workers engaged in the production of garments are paid fair wages and work in safe and healthy conditions.

Conscious clothing combats its evil twin sister, *fast fashion,* a business model emphasizing the quick turnover of clothing collections at affordable prices. This process was designed to encourage consumers to make frequent purchases. New styles are introduced and sold rapidly in response to consumption and the latest fashion trends, often relying on cheap labor and synthetic materials to keep costs low. If these issues are important to you, there are things you can do about it.

"Buy less and buy better" has become a common refrain. Simply wearing the clothes you own and only buying clothes you love is a big step in the right direction. You can also stay clear of fast fashion brands. More and more brands are making efforts to become more sustainable and ethical in their practices. If you have a favorite store or brand, check them out, learn about their practices, and think about that when you shop. Consider secondhand clothing. The number of quality consignment stores is exploding for local and online shoppers. If you haven't checked out Thredup, The RealReal, Tradesy, and Poshmark, these are large and successful options. The beauty of consignment stores is that you can purchase fabulous pre-owned items and trade in your own.

YOUR ULTIMATE STYLE BLUEPRINT

CULTURAL AND RELIGIOUS CONSIDERATIONS

What about cultural or religious dress requirements? You can build a wardrobe that inspires you no matter who you are and your belief system. I worked with two sisters who are Muslim. Both are successful and beautiful, yet struggled with feeling that way. They learned to dress their personal brand and Ultimate Style Blueprint with modesty, panache, and elegance. Take a look at Figures 13.1 and 13.2.

Before

After

Figure 13.1

Figure 13.2

SPECIALTY SIZING

Finally, many people need to consider specialty sizing. More and more stores have specialty sizing for petite, tall, and curvy individuals. Yet the fashion industry is not where it needs to be. If you require specialty sizing, your options can be limited. However, it is possible to find clothing that looks amazing on you. My recommendation for everyone is to buy timeless styles and quality items that can last for many years. This is even more

YOUR ULTIMATE STYLE BLUEPRINT

important if you are petite or tall and require alterations, or if you find it difficult to find styles you love that flatter you. The same is true for the larger or curvier guy or gal. The only exception is if you are on a weight-loss journey. In that case, you will likely want to buy clothes that are not investment pieces. You could purchase them secondhand or at a more affordable price. If you don't have more than a couple of sizes you wish to reduce, you can buy higher-priced items and alter them as you reach your ideal weight. My one caveat is *not* to wait until you are thin to invest in yourself. You deserve to look and feel fabulous at any size. Honor the body you have, and if you think a smaller version of yourself will boost your health and confidence, you can reassess your wardrobe when you reach your target weight.

The primary goal for all of this is to be intentional. Understand your Ultimate Style Blueprint, write everything down, create a plan, and only buy and wear things you love and that support your goals and lifestyle. One way to ensure you don't buy things you don't need is to become acutely aware of what you have. Check in with yourself when you are about to buy another pair of jeans or a cute top that looks like so many you already own. We are creatures of habit. You have likely read to this point because you are ready for a change. Make sure everything you wear and buy from this moment forward provides you joy, communicates who you are, and supports the you that you want to become.

CONCLUSION

To be yourself in a world that is constantly trying to make you something else is the greatest accomplishment.
—Ralph Waldo Emerson

Congratulations! You have embarked on a transformative journey and you are now equipped with the knowledge and tools to create a powerful visual identity that truly reflects who you are.

Throughout the book we've explored the profound impact of personal style and its ability to build self-confidence and attract success. In the first section, "Crafting Your Visual Identity: The Art of Personal Branding," you learned how your appearance is tied to self-confidence and influences how others perceive you. When you intentionally and artfully showcase your personality and values, you set the stage for a personal brand that portrays who you are with charisma and authenticity. In the second section, "The Art of Dressing for Your Unique Features," you learned how to use art and design concepts to showcase your best features. From embracing your shape and balancing your proportions to elevating your look with color and the right details, you gained the skills to celebrate your natural radiance. You now understand the artistry involved in accessorizing, selecting flattering hairstyles, and building a wardrobe that inspires confidence and success.

YOUR ULTIMATE STYLE BLUEPRINT

I have heard from clients that it can feel overwhelming as they begin to implement so much change. Remember, you don't have to do it all; you get to choose how much you want to implement and how quickly. Do you have to look perfect when you go to the grocery store, the gym, or your kids' soccer match? Of course not! The fact that we judge one another first based on how we look is true and indisputable. But we are human. Most of us don't have the time, energy, or inclination to implement perfection every day for every occasion. I ask you to pay attention to how you feel about yourself when you leave the house knowing you look your best. Let those emotions be your guide.

Learning to dress so you look amazing is accessible and achievable. It is not the definitive answer to living a life of complete self-confidence, but it is one of the easiest things you can do to feel great about yourself and show up in the world as the powerful, competent, and capable person you are on the inside. The goal is for your outside to match your inside and for you to achieve success through style.

Throughout the book, I have shared stories from some of my clients, men and women who felt held back for one reason or another and broke through their own personal barriers simply by changing how they looked. I hope for the same for you! As you move forward, keep these elements in mind:

- **Embrace your uniqueness**. Your individuality is your greatest asset. Celebrate what makes you different and let your style reflect your unique journey and personality.
- **Focus on self-confidence**. Confidence comes from within, but how you present yourself externally, how others respond to you, and how you feel when you see your reflection can significantly boost your self-assurance. Use your style to express your inner confidence and let it shine through in everything you do.
- **Continuously evolve.** Personal style is not static. As you grow and evolve, so too should your wardrobe. Stay open and

Conclusion

curious, experiment, and try not to simply follow fashion trends. Don't be afraid to reinvent yourself.
- **Achieve empowerment through knowledge**. You've learned not just what to wear but why it works for you. Follow your Ultimate Style Blueprint and trust yourself over the opinions of others.
- **Watch success follow**. Your appearance can open doors and create opportunities. By presenting yourself in a way that aligns with your goals, you will attract success and the attention of those who can help you achieve it.

This journey doesn't end here. Your style will continue to evolve as you do, and with the insights and strategies you've gained, you'll always have the tools to navigate the evolution with grace and confidence.

Thank you for allowing me to be a part of your style journey. Remember, the power of your image is in your hands. Go make your mark on the world looking and feeling your absolute best!

Stay in touch. Please visit my website at www.successthrustyle.com. Sign up for my newsletter at www.successthrustyle.com/newsletter. I often write with tips, success stories, new trends and advice, and occasional invitations to programs I offer. If you have a success story, please send it to cyndy@successthrustyle.com. I'd love to hear about it.

Here's to a confident, stylish, and successful future!

EPIGRAPH

Introduction: "*Why fit in when you were born to stand out?*" Dr. Seuss, Goodreads, accessed October 17, 2024, https://www.goodreads.com/quotes/187115-why-fit-in-when-you-were-born-to-stand-out.

Section 1: "*There's power in allowing yourself to be known and heard, in owning your unique story, in using your authentic voice,*" Michelle Obama, Goodreads, accessed October 17, 2024, https://www.goodreads.com/quotes/9679426-there-s-a-power-in-allowing-yourself-to-be-known-and.

Chapter 1: "*Self-confidence is like a superpower. Once you start to believe in yourself, magic starts to happen,*" Oscar Auliq-Ice, Goodreads, accessed October 17, 2024, https://www.goodreads.com/quotes/10886254-self-confidence-is-a-super-power-once-you-start-to.

Chapter 2: *"Clothes are to us as fur and feathers are to beasts and birds; they not only add to our appearance, but they are our appearance. How we look to others entirely depends upon what we wear and how we wear it. Manners and speech are noted afterward and character last of all,"* The Emily Post Institute, Facebook, accessed October 17, 2024, https://www.facebook.com/emilypostinstitute/photos/clothes-are-to-us-what-fur-and-feathers-are-to-beasts-and-birds-they-not-only-ad/10155414969471075/.

Chapter 3: *"An authentic and honest brand narrative is fundamental today; otherwise, you will simply be edited out,"* "19 Personal Branding Quotes to Inspire You," Wild Kind Photography, January 18, 2022, https://www.wildkindphotography.com/post/19-personal-brand-quotes-to-inspire-you.

Chapter 4: *"Be yourself; everyone else is already taken,"* Oscar Wilde, Goodreads, accessed October 17, 2024, https://www.goodreads.com/quotes/19884-be-yourself-everyone-else-is-already-taken.

Chapter 5: *"Style is a way to say who you are without having to speak,"* Rachel Zoe, Goodreads, accessed October 17, 2024, https://www.goodreads.com/quotes/635076-style-is-a-way-to-say-who-you-are-without.

Section II: *"The human form is the greatest masterpiece of art,"* commonly attributed to Michelangelo. While there is no verifiable source for this exact phrasing in his writings, it reflects the spirit of his work and philosophy, especially as seen in his sculptures like *David* and *The Creation of Adam*, where he celebrated the beauty and perfection of the human form.

Chapter 6: *"Finding tricks to create a flattering body shape is the key to style,"* Stacy London, BrainyQuote, accessed October 2024, https://www.brainyquote.com/quotes/stacy_london_531800, and AZQuotes, accessed October 2024, https://www.azquotes.com/quote/1017396.

Epigraphs

Chapter 7: *"Proportions are what make the old Greek temples classic in their beauty. It is the same with the human body; if the proportions are harmonious, the result is a great beauty,"* commonly attributed to Leonardo da Vinci. While there is no verifiable source for this exact phrasing in his documented works, it reflects his studies and philosophy, particularly seen in his illustration of the *Vitruvian Man* and his extensive work on human anatomy, where he explored the harmony between architectural and human proportions as a measure of beauty and perfection.

Chapter 8: *"I found I could say things with colors that I couldn't say in any other way—things I had no words for,"* Georgia O'Keeffe, BrainyQuote, accessed October 17, 2024, https://www.brainyquote.com/quotes/georgia_okeeffe_104135#:~:text=Georgia%20O'Keeffe%20Quotes&text=I%20found%20I%20could%20say%20things%20with%20color%20and%20shapes,I%20had%20no%20words%20for.

Chapter 9: *"The details are not the details. They make the design,"* Charles Eames, Goodreads, accessed October 17, 2024, https://www.goodreads.com/quotes/1052386-the-details-are-not-the-details-they-make-the-design.

Chapter 10: *"The face is a picture of the mind with the eyes as its interpreter,"* Marcus Tullius Cicero, *The Complete Works of Marcus Tullius Cicero* (Delphi Classics, 2014), p. 2599. Also referenced in "Soul-grippingly Beautiful Famous Quotes and Sayings About Eyes," Quotabulary, accessed October 2024, https://quotabulary.com/famous-quotes-sayings-about-eyes.

Chapter 11: *"I think the most important thing a woman can have next to her talent, of course, is her hairstylist,"* as cited in an interview with *Hollywood Reporter*, 1942, and Wikiquote, accessed October 2024, https://en.wikiquote.org/wiki/Joan_Crawford Wikiquote.

Chapter 12: *"Accessories are like the finishing strokes of a painter's brush. They highlight, define, and complete her masterpiece,"* Luly Yang, Medium, October 17, 2016, https://medium.com/@sophiafarnadiz/complete-your-look-with-a-colorful-bling-satchel-messenger-cross-body-bag-and-other-accessories-35705929a4f8.

Chapter 13: *"Any item in your wardrobe should satisfy one of two criteria: utility and joy,"* Stacy London, BrainyQuote, accessed October 17, 2024, https://routertest1.brainyquote.com/quotes/stacy_london_531809

Conclusion: *"To be yourself in a world that is constantly trying to make you something else is the greatest accomplishment,"* Ralph Waldo Emerson, Goodreads, accessed October 17, 2024, https://www.goodreads.com/quotes/876-to-be-yourself-in-a-world-that-is-constantly-trying

ENDNOTES

Chapter 1

1. Nancy Etcoff, Susie Orbach, Jennifer Scott, and Heidi D'Agostino, "The Real Truth About Beauty: A Global Report," commissioned by Dove, 2004, and "The Real Truth About Beauty: Revisited," 2010.

2. National Institutes of Health, "Your Healthiest Self: Wellness Toolkits," last reviewed May 19, 2023, https://www.nih.gov/health-information/your-healthiest-self-wellness-toolkits.

3. Hajo Adam and Adam D. Galinsky, "Enclothed Cognition," *Journal of Experimental Social Psychology* 48, no. 4 (2012): 918–925, https://doi.org/10.1016/j.jesp.2012.02.008.

4. Karen J. Pine, *Mind What You Wear: The Psychology of Fashion* (Amazon, 2014).

5. Pine, *Mind What You Wear*.

Chapter 2

1. Seth Stephens-Davidowitz, *Don't Trust Your Gut: Using Data to Get What You Really Want in Life* (New York: Dey Street Books, 2022).

2. Stephens-Davidowitz, *Don't Trust Your Gut.*

3. Ibid.

4. Ibid.

5. Alan M. Slater et al., "Newborn Infants Prefer Attractive Faces," *Infant Behavior and Development* 21, no. 4 (1998): 345–354.

6. Andrew Harrell, "Researchers Show Parents Give Unattractive Children Less Attention," *ScienceDaily*, April 13, 2005, https://www.sciencedaily.com/releases/2005/04/050412213412.htm.

7. Vedant Pradeep, ed., "What Is the Halo Effect?" *Reframe Blog*, accessed September 1, 2024, https://www.joinreframeapp.com/blog-post/what-is-the-halo-effect.

8. Janine Willis and Alexander Todorov, "First Impressions: Making Up Your Mind After a 100-Ms Exposure to a Face," *Psychological Science* 17, no. 7 (2006): 592–598.

9. Konstantin Tskhay et al., "Perceptions of Charisma from Thin Slices of Nonverbal Behavior," *Journal of Personality and Social Psychology* 113, no. 6 (2017): 775–791.

10. Rob M.A. Nelissen and Marijn H.C. Meijers, "Social Benefits of Luxury Brands as Costly Signals of Wealth and Status," *Evolution and Human Behavior* 32, no. 5 (2011): 343–355.

11. "Tailored Suit vs. Off the Rack – Which Is Best?" *Male Mode*, April 5, 2017, https://male-mode.com/2017/04/tailored-suit-vs-off-rack-best/.

12. Albert Mannes, "Shorn Scalps and Perceptions of Male Dominance," *Social Psychological and Personality Science* 4, no. 2 (2012): 198–205.

13. Brett and Kate McKay, "Why Your First Impression Matters," *The Art of Manliness*, November 3, 2016; last updated July 2, 2023, https://www.artofmanliness.com/character/behavior/surprising-importance-first-impression/.

Endnotes

Chapter 3

1. Andy Ackerman, Seinfeld, Season 5, Episode 22, "The Summer of George," aired May 20, 1994, on NBC.

2. Julie Mazziotta, "Serena Williams Knows She's Been on 'Worst Dressed Lists' and Thinks It's 'Important'—Here's Why," *People*, April 11, 2024, https://people.com/serena-williams-important-being-on-worst-dressed-lists-50th-exclusive-8629943.

3. Meg Walters, "Serena Williams' Most Iconic Outfits Ever," *The List*, September 9, 2022, https://www.thelist.com/1001282/serena-williams-most-iconic-outfits-ever/; Vatsal Shah, "Created a New Culture in Tennis—Nike's Vice President Once Revealed How Serena Williams Created an Inspiring Legacy," *Essentially Sports*, August 21, 2022, https://www.essentiallysports.com/wta-tennis-news-created-a-new-culture-in-tennis-nikes-vice-president-once-revealed-how-serena-williams-created-an-inspiring-legacy/; "How Serena Williams Won the Fashion Game," *Godfrey Times*, September 1, 2022 (page no longer available).

4. Andre Agassi, *Open: An Autobiography* (New York: Vintage Books, 2010).

5. Albert Mehrabian, *Silent Messages* (Belmont, CA: Wadsworth Publishing Company, 1971).

6. Dianna Dilworth, "The Most Loved Brands of 2022," *Brand Innovators*, June 13, 2022, https://www.brand-innovators.com/news/the-most-loved-brands-of-2022/.

Chapter 4

1. Life is Good, "Our Story," accessed June 17, 2024, https://www.lifeisgood.com/our-story.html.

2. Warby Parker, "Buy a Pair, Give a Pair," accessed August 2, 2024, https://investors.warbyparker.com/overview/.

3. American Express, "About Us," accessed June 17, 2024, https://www.americanexpress.com/in/company/mission.html

4. Nordstrom, "About Us," accessed June 17, 2024, https://shop.nordstrom.com/c/about-us.

5. M.K. Gandhi, The Mind of Mahatma Gandhi (Rajpal & Sons, 1967), 106.

6. Disney, Walt. The American Weekly. 1954.

7. Goodreads, "Maya Angelou Quotes," accessed June 17, 2024, https://www.goodreads.com/quotes/11877-my-mission-in-life-is-not-merely-to-survive-but.

Chapter 5

1. Alyce Parsons, *StyleSource: The Power of the Seven Universal Styles for Women and Men* (Universal Style International, 2008).

2. House of Colour, "Personal Style Analysis," accessed July 12, 2024, https://www.houseofcolour.co.uk.

Chapter 6

1. Africa Studio/Illustration of golden ratio in nature/Shutterstock/ accessed October 10, 2019, https://www.shutterstock.com; Leonardo da Vinci/Mona Lisa with Golden Ratio overlay/Wikimedia Commons, accessed July 15, 2024, https://commons.wikimedia.org/wiki/File:Mona_Lisa_Golden_Ratio.jpg.

2. Superdrug, "Perceptions of Perfection," accessed June 17, 2024, https://onlinedoctor.superdrug.com/perceptions-of-perfection.html.

3. Superdrug, "Perceptions of Perfection, Part II: Men," accessed June 17, 2024, https://onlinedoctor.superdrug.com/perceptions-of-perfection-part-ii-men.html.

4. Cindy Istook, "Fashion Designers Ignoring Shapes of Women's Bodies," *Newswise*, February 20, 2006, accessed June 17, 2024, https://www.newswise.com/articles/fashion-designers-ignoring-shapes-of-womens-bodies.

Chapter 7

1. Leonardo da Vinci, Image of Vitruvian Man, Canva, accessed July 21, 2024; used under license.

Endnotes

2. Leonardo da Vinci, *Vitruvian Man,* c. 1490, accessed June 17, 2024, There is a translated version of Leonardo's original notes with this measurement in The Notebooks of Leonardo Da Vinci, Vol. 1, Dover Publications, pp. 182-183, where it discusses proportions including this "one-eighth" measurement for the head height relative to the whole body.

Chapter 8

1. Johann Wolfgang von Goethe, *Theory of Colours,* c. 1809–1810, pen and black ink, watercolor on yellowish paper, mounted on cardboard, Frankfurt Goethe Museum, Wikimedia Commons, accessed July 21, 2020, https://commons.wikimedia.org/wiki/File:Goethe,_Farbenkreis_zur_Symbolisierung_des_menschlichen_Geistes-_und_Seelenlebens,_1809.jpg.

Chapter 10

1. Richard Corson, *Fashions in Makeup: From Ancient to Modern Times* (London: Peter Owen, 1972).

2. L'Oréal, "Our Brands," accessed June 17, 2024, https://www.loreal.com/brand.

3. Estée Lauder Companies, "Our Brands," accessed June 17, 2024, https://www.elcompanies.com/en/our-brands.

4. Procter & Gamble, "Our Brands," accessed June 17, 2024, https://us.pg.com/brands/.

ABOUT THE AUTHOR

Cyndy Porter is the founder and principal at Success thru Style. Her company and career have transitioned and grown to match her insatiable passion for helping people look and feel confident and succeed on their own terms.

She received her degree in marketing from California State University, Chico. She spent twenty years as a sales and marketing professional in high-tech companies. Her stops included WAIS (Wide Area Information Server, one of the first Internet companies in existence) and Kodak. Her final stop on the corporate ladder was as a divisional vice president of marketing at America Online (AOL).

Thereafter, Cyndy became an award-winning professional photographer and certified image consultant. Her mission is to help women look and feel beautiful, confident, and powerful. (She works with men too!) Her clients have gone on to start their own businesses, multiply their incomes, change careers, be promoted, and forge healthy relationships.

Cyndy lives in greater Washington, DC, with her husband, Jack; dog, Zoey; and, when she's lucky, her son, Steven, who is attending college in Chicago.

www.ingramcontent.com/pod-product-compliance
Lightning Source LLC
LaVergne TN
LVHW061532070526
838199LV00034B/641/J